The Flint Street Nativity

A comedy with music

Tim Firth

Samuel French — London
www.samuelfrench-london.co.uk

THE FLINT STREET NATIVITY

Adapted from a play for television and first produced for stage by the Everyman Liverpool Playhouse on the 28th December 2006 with the following cast:

Innkeeper	Andrew Schofield
Mary	Gillian Kearney
Wise Gold	Annabelle Dowler
Shepherd	Natalie Casey
Gabriel	Leanne Best
Star of Bethlehem/Ass	Nick Bagnall
Angel	Rina Mahoney
Narrator	Paul Kemp
Herod/Joseph	Neil Caple
Wise Frankincense	John Marquez

Director Matthew Lloyd
Designer Robin Don
Lighting Charles Balfour
Sound John Leonard
Musical Director Gavin Kaufman
AV Designer Chris O'Neil

CHARACTERS

Boys
Innkeeper
Star
Ass
Narrator
Herod/Joseph
Wise Frankincense
Shepherd

Girls
Mary
Wise Gold
Angel
Gabriel
Shepherd

SYNOPSIS OF SCENES

ACT I

SCENE 1	Mrs Horrocks' Classroom
SCENE 2	Mrs Horrocks' Special Place
SCENE 3	The Wings
SCENE 4	The Stage
SCENE 5	The Playground
SCENE 6	The Wings
SCENE 7	The Stage

ACT II

Scene 1	The Stage
SCENE 2	Mrs Horrocks' Special Place
Scene 3	The Stage
SCENE 4	The Playground
SCENE 5	The Wings
SCENE 6	Mrs Horrocks' Special Place
SCENE 7	The Stage
SCENE 8	Mrs Horrocks' Special Place
SCENE 9	Stage and wings
SCENE 10	Mrs Horrocks' Adult Size Classroom
SCENE 11	The Playground
SCENE 12	Mrs Horrocks' Classroom

MUSICAL NUMBERS

ACT 1

No 1	Something About Virgins	Everyone
No 2	My House Always Smells Of Beer	Innkeeper
No 3	Don't Grow Up Like Your Dad	Star and Everyone
No 4	A Way To Kill Mary	Mary and Gabriel
No 5	Watch How Mummy Does It	Mary and Herod and Chorus

ACT II

No 6	Shiny Silver Caravan	Shepherd and Everyone
No 7	If There Was A God	Ass and Wise Frankincense
No 8	Lucky Lady	Wise Gold, Angel, Narrator and Everyone
No 9	Massive Newt	Everyone
No 10	I Wish	Everyone

The piano/vocal score is available on hire from:

SAMUEL FRENCH LTD, 52 FITZROY STREET, LONDON W1T 5JR

AUTHOR'S NOTE

The first act comprises activity in the childrens' classroom prior to the performance and the first part of the nativity proper. The second act concludes the nativity proper then returns us to the classroom, only this time at the scale of adult, the actors now playing the part of their respective child's parent.

Describing action in a busy infant classroom is of course like trying to describe the structure of a vegetable soup. Conversations swirl around, occasionally interlocking, sometimes occurring almost simultaneously in more than one location.

For ease of navigation through this soup the single set of Mrs Horrocks' classroom is sometimes subdivided into different 'areas' if it's vital that dialogue takes place in these areas. If it isn't, then it could take place anywhere.

Never has the word 'deadpan' been more apposite than when describing the comedy of children. They are never aware of their humour in this play. The less funny they find it, the funnier it will be.

The style should take its tone from the most gritty naturalism of adult dramas which have dealt with similar brutality, as *Goodfellas* or *The Godfather*.

Basically, the playing should be as realistic as the situations would seem for those kids involved. The more real, the more pointed it is.

STAGING NOTES

Part of the challenge of *The Flint Street Nativity* is the creation of the scaled props and classroom. The only direct prerequisite is that there be a small flight of steps leading from classroom floor up to the acting area of the stage, the ones that Herod will attempt to scale from inside his cape in the second act.

The major coup of course is turning one scale into the other, moving from the world of children to that of adults. In the original production this challenge was ingeniously met by Robin Don. The stage on which the nativity is performed was placed up a small set of steps; at the crucial moment, this whole module separated to reveal the same classroom, only now of adult scale, hidden behind it.

As ever, there will be other ways in which an inspired designer can pull off this coup. The key is to allow it its own little moment of glory and relish the theatre of the reveal, rather than attempting some fast cinematic cut.

MAKING FLINT STREET *YOUR* STREET

It is vital that the play is thoroughly owned by the area in which it is performed. To this end there are a small number of direct local references which should be tweaked to make it feel that Flint Street Primary could be a school the audience had unwittingly walked past to get to the theatre. The list is as follows:

page 4.   Peter Crouch — anyone famous enough for kids to know, who is tall and noticeably thin of stature. Peter may suffice for a long time in this role. If there are local alternatives, use them.

page 5.   JRL Sports Liverpool Half Marathon — replace Liverpool with local city capable of hosting such an event

page 5.   Maghull — nearby small town with dull name

page 6.   Westlife — mass-appeal kid-friendly pop band of the day

page 6.   Netto — Local own-brand, low-priced supermarket

page 6.   Flint Street — this can remain Flint Street as a generic street name or be customized to a known area or road in the region

page 6.   Poundstretcher — local budget shop

page 7.   Question of Sport/Ally/Sue — the tv sports quiz of the day, which probably for a long time will remain the BBC's *A Question of Sport*. The host, Sue, and a team leader, Phil Tuffnell, may well vary over time.

page 8.   Nugget — local playground insult of the day

page 11. Ernie Els — contemporary sportsman with unromantic name

page 13. Morecambe — nearby resort of limited ambition

page 24. Hope University — local university, ideally of one syllable length In the song you can get away with two syllables at a pinch and three at a push.

page 46. Matalan — this may remain for centuries as a budget clothing giant. Should it not, use whatever locally replaces it.

page 47. Jordan — female glamour figure of the day

page 52. Brannigan's — local pub chain or nightclub

page 54. The Empire — local commercial large-scale theatre house

page 64. John Prescott — local overweight public figure, preferably a politician.

Finally, thanks are due to Peter Elias-Jones for producing the original TV film, Marcus Mortimer for directing it, and to a combination of Geoff Edkins, Suzanne Bell, Deborah Aydon and Gemma Bodinetz for seeing potential in the stage version. Also to Gavin Kaufman for his crucial help preparing the piano score.

Tim Firth

Photograph by Robin Don

Photograph by Robin Don

Other plays by Tim Firth
published by Samuel French Ltd

Calendar Girls
The End of the Food Chain
A Man of Letters
Neville's Island
The Safari Party
Sign of the Times

ACT I

Scene 1

Mrs Horrocks' classroom

The front cloth is liveried with a Victorian junior school and the graffiti: "The Flint Street Nativity".

From within are the unmistakable sounds of children 'happily playing'

There is a tambourine shake and slap

Sudden silence. The cloth goes up to reveal a group of seven year olds standing in a clump staring directly at the audience. Here are Mary, Herod, Gabriel, Innkeeper, Shepherd, Wise Man Gold, Wise Man Frankincense, the Star of Bethlehem, Angel, and Narrator

The group are all pinned like escaping convicts by a fierce, very defined white spotlight. This is the gaze of their teacher, Mrs Horrocks

Behind them is a teacher's chair which dwarfs them, and to one side a swing bin which also dwarfs them. They are variously holding art material rubbish: a cornflake box, a roll of silver foil, an egg carton. These have clearly gone into the recent making of a star on a hook which looks like a glitterball, and which one of them is holding

They are, by the way, in a distinctly Victorian infant school classroom with high windows designed so kids couldn't be distracted by thoughts of freedom whilst working. Through the main window at the back we can see the top of some brightly-painted playground apparatus

The room has a raised stage at the back with the Home Corner on it, accessed by steps on both sides, and in front of that, some of the debris of a normal classroom. This includes tables, chairs, and a nature table with a plastic stick insect tank on it. There is also an interest area with an astronaut suit and a sign saying "Marcus's uncle works for NASA", with various photos to substantiate this claim. On the art wall are several children's paintings of the nativity. On the "Who's Been Good?" chart, no-one has more than two stars, except for Jenny, who has twelve. Next to Bradley has been written: "I have".

The children just stare right at the audience. They do nothing but hold their rubbish. Absolutely nothing. This goes on for a good few seconds. Then they suddenly all nod. Mary leads this. Mary leads everything. The nodding stops. Suddenly everyone shakes their heads. Then this stops. Then everyone points at the Innkeeper

Innkeeper (*fiercely*) I never. I didn't. I never. I——

Suddenly the white light snaps to red, accompanied by a tambourine struck against a hand, which Mrs Horrocks uses to warn of a coming ill — like a rattlesnake

The Innkeeper jerks his finger on his lips and shuts up

(*Muttering*) Sorry, Missis Horrocks.

This causes the red light to go back to white

(*Dropping his finger from his lips; muttering*) Never.

The light snaps to red again for a second. The Innkeeper jerks his finger back to his lips. Several hands go up. Who's first? Surprise, surprise, it's Mary

Mary Yes. We all have to look at the clock and sing clearly and not go (*as if singing without knowing the words*) Mrrrrlllrrr.

Pause. Mary looks around. Clearly, no-one else knows the answer, so she puts her hand up again

We won't need the carol words on the overhead projector because we've all taken them home and learned them all off by heart.

There is a pause as all the other kids turn slowly to look at Mary. It is immediately clear this point is doubtful

The Wise Man Gold puts her hand up and down

Wise Gold Can I? Mizz Horrocks? If Darren's got chickenpox, can I do the myrrh as well?

Shepherd (*hand up*) Mizz Horrocks? My dad says at the end if we all have to carry flags from the children of the world, can ours not be France please, 'cause the French are a load of — shttp.

The teacher light snaps to red, causing Shepherd's finger to shoot up to her lips

Mary (*nodding*) Practice. (*Relaying to those around her*) Practice. We have to practice a carol. You stand there.

This continues as the piano starts the introduction to...

Music 1. Something About Virgins

Everyone shuffles ready for take-off

Everyone (*with some gusto*) O come, all ye faithful.

Mary carries on, loud and true. Everyone else instantly has no idea of the words, and descends into the usual mush

Mary	**Everyone else**
Joyful and triumphant.	nmm rrr mmr hmm brmm mmm
O come ye, o come ye	nrr brr rrrh mrr car brr mmm

Ah, here's a bit they all know (together; with gusto)

To Be-ethlehem.	To Be-ethlehem.

As they continue, everyone else looks at Mary, as she sings the right words

Mary	**Everyone else** (*singing the wrong words*)
Come and behold him	I wish I'd learned my
Born the King of Angels	Words like Jenny Bennet has.
O come let us adore him.	I wish that I had learned them.
O come let us adore him.	Miss Horrocks said to learn them
O come let us adore him	I didn't, so I just go hrr
Christ the Lord.	mrrr-rr-ne-nurr.

Mary continues to sing a virtual solo in the background, becoming a quiet underscore to everyone else

The other kids look up, around, anywhere, losing interest in the song

Mary (sotto voce)	**Wise Frankincense** (*lisping*)
True God of true God,	True God of thomething.
Light from Light Eternal.	**Gabriel** Something about virgins.
Lo, he shuns not the	**Herod** Mum said to ask my dad what
Virgin's womb.	virgins are.
Son of the Father,	**Narrator & Star** My uncle, Ted, flies
Begotten not created.	Virgins to America.
O come let us adore him.	**Innkeeper** I like this where we go quiet.
	Everyone Shh.

O come let us adore him.　　　**Innkeeper** And then we get much louder.
　　　　　　　　　　　　　　　　Everyone Shh.
O come let us adore him　　　**Innkeeper** (*shouting*) And then they let us
　　　　　　　　　　　　　　　　shout.

The red teacher light shines on the Innkeeper. All the other kids turn to look at him

Christ the Lord.　　　　　　　**Everyone else** Bradley's got done.

The Innkeeper is clearly "sent off" and trudges up to the Home Corner, once inside of which he shuts the door

The other kids start, one by one, to put their hands to one ear in replication of Mrs Horrocks doing it

Mary (sotto voce)　　　　　　**Wise Gold** ⎫
　Sing, choirs of angels,　　　　**Angel** 　　⎬ (*together*)　Why has Miss
　Sing in exultation;　　　　　　　　　　⎭　　Horrocks
　　　　　　　　　　　　　　　　Started doing that now?

　　　　　　　　　　　　　　　　*They all point to their mouths, doing
　　　　　　　　　　　　　　　　excessively exaggerated mouth movements*

Sing, all ye citizens of　　　　**Everyone** Whyy izzz Miss Horrocks dooing
Heaven above.　　　　　　　　　Tharrt weeth herr mouth?
Glory to God,　　　　　　　　**Shepherd** If she's a lady
All glory in the highest.　　　　Why's she got a hairy lip?

O come let us adore him.　　　**Narrator** ⎫
　　　　　　　　　　　　　　　Star 　　⎬ (*together*) Jesus had a moustache.

O come let us adore him.　　　**Gabriel** ⎫
　　　　　　　　　　　　　　　Herod 　 ⎬ (*together*) Miss Horrocks has a
　　　　　　　　　　　　　　　　　　　　moustache.

O come let us adore him　　　**Everyone** So maybe Missis Horrocks is
Christ the Lord.　　　　　　　Christ the Lord.

Immediately the song ends, all hands fly up to ask various questions

Everyone (*variously*) Mrs Horrocks! Mrs Horrocks!

But Mrs Horrocks has gone. No worry

Mary (*taking control*) Yes, Miss Horrocks. Move tables ready for the mums' and dads' chairs. (*Nodding and pointing*) Miss Horrocks wants... Peter Crouch needs moving, but no goin' in the special cupboard. Marcus, move the spacesuit. Tim you look after new Adrian. I'll get Jesus. Ryan, learn what Joseph says and comb y'r hair. And all stuff from making the star goes in the bin.

Hand-held debris is put in the swing bin by Wise Frankincense, Joseph, Shepherd and Narrator

Wise Frankincense, Joseph, Shepherd, Narrator and Herod exit

Ashley?
Gabriel We all heard.

Star busies himself taking down the astronaut suit. He is carrying a silver-sprayed cardboard star and is wrapped in a thermal blanket which reads "JRL Sports Liverpool Half Marathon"

Star It's not a proper star, this. What Missis Horrocks wants to come up over Bethlehem. *That* isn't. (*Indicating the pointy silver one they've just made*) 'Cause stars don't have (*waving at its "starry" points*) all that comin' off. My uncle works for NASA an' he gave me a wallchart and this, right... (*indicating his graphically accurate one, on his head*) ...this is Sirius. This actually IS Sirius. But Missis Horrocks says it might be a star but it doesn't look like one an' I can't go up the rope anyway 'cause they don't let kids up ropes since that boy in Maghull fell off a climbing rope an' his leg came out through his bum.

Gabriel (*with the dead-eyed steel of a mafia boss*) Shamima. Get Jesus.

Angel and Wise Gold instinctively look to Mary, who has sat down and got out her Jesus and started to brush his hair

Wise Gold There's Jesus.
Gabriel (*deadly*) The other Jesus.

Angel and Wise Gold immediately go scurrying off and exit to the girls' cloakroom

Star Did y' know? That's... (*pointing to display*) My " Uncle Ted works for NASA". This (*pointing to his head*) is actually Sirius, which is...

The Narrator enters from the boys' toilets. He is the only one in school uniform, albeit it somewhat shabby and long-trousered. He has large pieces of cardboard with his words Sellotaped on

(*No breath taken, to the Narrator now*) It's not a star proper, that, 'cause of having these (*gesturing the "spikes"*) comin' off.

Angel sticks her head round from the girls' toilets

Angel Is Jesus in the Westlife bag or the Netto bag?
Gabriel (*staring out like the godfather*) Westlife.
Narrator (*giving speech-cards to Mary*) Hold them, will y'?
Star (*to Gabriel*) They've got a Jesus. What are you?
Gabriel (*staring at Mary*) Gonna be Mary.
Star I thought you were the Angel Gabriel.
Gabriel I am. But I'm gonna be Mary.
Narrator (*closing his eyes*) "Welcome to the Flint Street Nativity."
Star Y'know Declan who was gonna be Joseph? He was sick. In a sock.
Narrator "We were hoping..."
Star My mum met his mum in Poundstretcher.
Narrator (*sneaking look at card*) Let us see it again.
Mary What y' doing?
Narrator Me words. (*Showing Mary*) Gonna know all me words so I can
show me dad.

*The daisy-henchmen, Angel and Wise Gold, enter from the girls toilets
and present Gabriel with a baby Jesus, also in a shawl, and a comb*

Mary Ryan won't know his words.
Narrator (*peeking another crib*) Let us see.
Mary He was just Herod but now he's got to do Joseph as well 'cause of
Declan having chickenpox, and he won't know his words.
Narrator If you know the words...
Mary Not without looking down, and you're not allowed. (*She rises*) He'll
have to practice.
Narrator People are proud. Mrs Horrocks said she'd be proud if we learnt
all the words to the carols. It makes people proud.

Mary looks at him a beat

Narrator My dad's coming.
Star Voyager Ten. This is NASA to Voyager Ten.

Mary puts down baby Jesus and exits in search of Herod/Joseph

Star recreates a NASA flight with a model space shuttle

Narrator "We are in Mrs Horrocks' classroom again this year because the builders diggin' the new school hall found some Great Crested Newts which means they have to (*reading it with difficulty*) notify the environment agency."

Wise Gold can't help noticing the baby left behind

Wise Gold Ashley?
Star (*into the stick insect tank*) Everyone's dead, over. Everyone on 'ere's dead with red hangin' out.

Herod mooches in and, during the following, installs himself at a chair and table, rather like a TV panel show host

Star Monster was on here with teeth, an' he opened it, an' there was more teeth on his tongue. (*He does an "Alien"*) Yash yash.
Wise Gold (*to Gabriel, smiling and wincing simultaneously*) Is that Jesus?
Gabriel (*combing baby Jesus' hair. Pause. Comb, comb*) This is Jesus.
Wise Gold (*looking at the Jesus which Mary left*) Isn't there already a Jesus?
Gabriel This is Jesus. (*Pause, comb, comb*)
Wise Gold Isn't Jenny Bennet Mary and...
Gabriel SAY HALLO JESUS.
Wise Gold Hallo Jesus.
Herod (*singing the "A Question of Sport" theme*) La laaa laarrr nurr nuh-nuh. Clap clap clap. (*He claps*) Hallo. And welcome to Question of Sport. Ally McCoist, pick a number. (*He changes voice slightly — it's not good enough to be an "impression"*) Ooooo er now... (*Scratching his head*) Let's see. Number nine. (*Changing his voice slightly*) Number nine, now John, who is that? (*Changing his voice slightly*) How the hell do I know, Sue?

Pause for huge comic effect

He's got a hat on! (*Going immediately serious, like a producer in an edit*) Laughs now. Ha ha. Laugh, laugh, laugh.

Mary enters and spies Herod, her prey, whom she joins

Wise Gold wanders off to survey some of the nativity pictures on the wall

Angel notices that Wise Gold has gone, and has instinctively been drawn away from the "godfather" Gabriel to comfort Wise Gold after being shouted at

Angel (*pointing out a picture*) That's mine. (*Pointing out characters on the painting*) Jesus. Mary. Wise Man. Is that you?

Wise Gold is too hurt to respond

Angel Jess? What are you?
Gabriel (*combing Jesus; without turning*) Fat cow.
Wise Gold Wise man.
Gabriel Fat man. She's a fat man. Isn't she Shamima?
Angel (*calling*) Yeah. (*To Wise Gold*) Sorry.
Wise Gold S' OK.
Star (*knocking on the door of the Home Corner with some trepidation*) Bradley?

Mary is trying to comb Herod's hair from under the crown on his head

Herod Get lost, y' nugget.
Mary You 'ave to! Y' should be learnin' — was that you learnin' y'r words then?
Herod I was playin' the "Question of Sport" game. (*Batting her hand off*) Get ——
Mary What?
Herod Like on the telly.
Mary What game?
Herod I made it up. What y' do is you sit down... (*That's it, really*)
Mary And then what?
Herod Y'do "Question of Sport" like it is on the telly.
Mary (*grabbing him*) Come here.
Herod (*knocking her hand away*) Look I'm havin' a crown.
Mary Not when y'r Joseph y'r not!
Herod I don't wanna be Joseph. Joseph's a nugget.
Mary It won't look — Ryan-n! My dad, when he got married, OK there's photos everywhere, to my mum, and his hair is flat, OK. It's *flat*. It's dead, totally, completely — D'you know your words without looking?
Star (*aware his actions are dangerous*) Bradley—y? Bradley—y? Are you ——? (*Jumping but quietly*) Argh.

The door opens. The Innkeeper is there, like something from a Hitchcock film. Eerie music accompanies this. It is the music of what Star feels in his heart

(*Mouth instantly dry*) We have — we — we have to move Peter Crouch.

The Innkeeper's look is deathly, his silence crippling

For the nativity. So he dun't get knocked. Miss Horrocks said.

Nothing

(*Gesturing feebly*) Round the corner. Now. Sort of.

The Innkeeper emerges, slowly, like a gangster and stands

(*In meltdown*) Are y' comin'...? Are we goin'...?

The Innkeeper gives the tiniest of head-flicks, suggesting Star gets moving

We're goin'. Right.

Star shoots off to the nature table, the Innkeeper follows him, walking in his own time

Wise Gold and Angel are still inspecting pictures on the picture wall

Wise Gold (*indicating characters*) This one's got Jesus. Donkey. (*Next one*) Jesus. Mary. Donkey.
Angel (*pointing out another painting*) Jesus. Joseph. Fat man. Donkey.
Wise Gold (*pointing out another painting*) Duck with an ice cream.
Angel That's Moira's. She's Jehovah's Witness. She said she can't do Christmas or assembly or anything so Mizz Horrocks just told her to paint something happy.
Star (*rotating, asteroid-like, round the cool, malevolent Innkeeper*) What it is, right, it looks like a stick an' what that is, right, that's when like things, yeah, that might eat them, when things go past they think "Oh, that's a stick down there. That's just — I'm not eating that, that is definitely just a——"
Innkeeper (*quietly*) Pick it up.

Pause

Star (*same volume, trying to avoid the challenge*) —Definitely just a stick". An' where my uncle lives, in (*nodding*) in Florida, Ted, they have stick insects (*indicating a rather unlikely size*) that big.
Innkeeper Dares y'.
Star Where the rockets... (*blinking*) He's coming for Christmas.
Innkeeper (*shark-eyed, slowly*) Dares y'.

Pause

Star (*almost inaudibly*) Virgin seven-four-seven.

The Innkeeper kills him with a look and thrusts his own hand into the tank

(*Like an ITN war correspondent*) Peter Crouch! He's — oh, he's — Bradley's getting Peter Crouch out!

Mary reacts instantly and walks off at some pace

Mary (*petrified; to herself, as she goes*) No, no, no, no.
Star He's out! He's got Peter Crouch out!

Gabriel doesn't miss a beat of Mary's discomfort

Mary heads out past the incoming Wise Frankincense in his Laura Ashley curtains. He is a slightly posher kid, but has a slight lisp

Wise Frankincense We have to move Mith Horrock's chair into the... Whoa no! Peter Crouch! (*Turning randomly*) Mith Horrocks!

Wise Frankincense exits immediately

Gabriel Eh. When she comes back, get Jenny Bennet an' show her that, right up here. (*He gestures "dead close"*) She loves crawly insects. People who can pick 'em up and put 'em right up here.
Star (*on auto pilot*) My Uncle Ted's coming tomorrow.

Innkeeper brusquely puts the insect back and eyeballs Star

Innkeeper (*nodding at the insect*) You. Now. Miss Horrock's special cupboard. (*He gets behind the insect trolley; challenging Star*) Dares y'.

Star and Innkeeper wheel the insect trolley off and exit

Star (*trailing off*) My Uncle Ted is...
Angel (*pointing at another painting*) Is that Gabriel?
Wise Gold That's Angel Gabriel. I did Gabriel because she's one of the angels who ——
Gabriel (*snapping*) It's not "one of the angels". It's the number one angel. Gabriel is boss of all the angels. He was absolute... all the others— he was the very...absolute... (*She searches for a higher rank, mouths a couple to try them out, then gives up*) Shamima. Let's not talk to Jess.

Gabriel waltzes out with the baby Jesus

Wise Frankincense enters

Angel flicks a shrug smile at Wise Gold, but she's been summoned by 'the almighty'

Angel exits after Gabriel

Wise Gold is left behind and looks stricken

Narrator "In the fields around Bethlehem there were some shepherds."
Wise Frankincense (*nudging Narrator*) We have to put Miss Horrocks' chair in the corridor. (*He starts collecting chairs*)
Narrator (*closing his eyes*) "An angel came down, and——
Wise Frankincense (*badgering Narrator*) We have to put Miss Horrocks' chair in——
Narrator ——and the shepherds were sore... The Shepherds had sores. I'm afraid."

The Shepherd enters. She is a brutally factual girl with a Spanish straw donkey which has a lascivious wink and a sombrero

Shepherd Right.
Herod (*still conferring in his game*) He dun't believe me. He dun't believe — I told y' it was Ernie Els!
Shepherd Donkey.
Herod (*going dead serious again*) Laugh, laugh, laugh.
Shepherd This is y'r donkey, right, an' you don't pull his ears.
Herod Herod dun't 'ave a donkey.
Shepherd Yeah well, Joseph has a donkey, an' you're Joseph an' all now so you have to 'ave him an' y'don't pull his ears, or he says rude things in Spanish, an' y'don't tell Miss Horrocks that either, or she won't let him be the donkey.
Herod (*different voice*) Yes, that's correct. It was indeed Ernie Els at the American open in Augusta. Two points Ally.

Wise Frankincense gravitates in

Wise Frankincense What'th hith name?
Shepherd Mum calls her Sparkle but if you turn that (*turning the saddle cloth*) the other way it says "Dirty Pedro".
Herod Clap clap clap.
Wise Frankincense I've been to Thpain.
Shepherd (*frowning at that word*) You've been to what?

Wise Frankincense becomes immediately panicked about his lisp

Wise Frankincense (*dodging the subject*) We don't have them, you thee.
We give him prethenth.
Shepherd (*frowning again*) You give him what?
Wise Frankincense (*sweating*) We used to have a house in Thpain.
Shepherd Where you come from do they all talk like you?
Wise Frankincense Daddy playth golf. There's hith name on a board.
Shepherd (*staring into Wise Frankincense's mouth*) Is there summat
wrong wi' your mouth?
Wise Frankincense Where we uth-ed to live, my dad wath captain of all
golf.

Pause

(*Bottling*) Have to move the chair.

*Wise Frankincense exits. Ass enters, passing Wise Frankincense on the
way. This is a boy in a shabby school uniform, his own head obscured by
a donkey's head made out of painted cereal packets. His energy is that of
someone who doesn't give a toss and slightly shouts most things*

Narrator "There appeared above them all the beautiful star of Bethlehem."
(*He checks his accuracy against the prompt cards*)

Wise Gold stands, rudderless and friendless

Herod (*continuing his show with another voice*) We'll go for number five,
Sue. (*Conferring*) Mnnnnnnrgggrrrmmm...

The Shepherd is combing the mane of her clopping donkey

Ass joins Herod and sits next to him during the following speech

(*To camera*) We think-k... Tiger Woods. (*He pauses then throws
hands in the air*) Yes! (*He claps, dead serious*) Clap-p. Clap. Clap.
Clap. (*Turning back to his imaginary team mate*) Mmmmmrrrrm-
mmm. Ahaha ha ha. Laugh, laugh, la—— (*He turns back to find his
co-panellist is now Ass*)
Ass (*always slightly shouting*) 'E's not a proper donkey.
Herod (*grimly*) Y'r sitting on Ally McCoist.

His voice echoes inside his head. He points to "Pedro"

Shepherd 'E is a proper donkey.
Wise Gold (*gravitating for company*) He's from Spain. I've been to Spain!

Shepherd You're not a proper donkey. You just got a donkey 'ead.
Wise Gold We always go. We go at weekends.
Shepherd Y'can't go t' Spain f'r weekends.
Wise Gold (*swallowing*) Y'can.
Shepherd Can't.
Wise Gold Y' can, but... (*Struggling*) ...it's a special bit of Spain.
Shepherd Where?
Wise Gold Morecambe.

Shepherd retreats to the picture wall

Herod Who is it, Sue? (*Changing voice*) Have to hurry you. (*Changing voice back*) Don't do this to me. (*Changing voice again*) Have to hurry you-u.
Ass (*inside the mask*) CAN I BE IN IT?

Herod grudgingly turns

Herod Dunno how to play.
Ass (*nodding*) I DO.
Herod This game?
Ass (*nodding*) YES.
Herod With the sportsmen.
Ass (*nodding*) YES.

Herod evaluates whether he should give the Ass an inch, and decides to

Herod OK. (*Assuming question master's role*) Phil. Who in nineteen seventy-two won seven Olympic golds for swimming?
Ass MY DAD.
Herod (*instantly pointing for him to leave*) Off you go.
Ass (*standing*) OK.

As Ass stands, Wise Gold attempts friendship with the departing Shepherd

Wise Gold Zoe? That's yours! (*Pointing at a picture*) That picture. Isn't it. That's good, that one. It's the best. With Joseph and Mary and the fat man. Can I sit with you in Bethlehem?
Shepherd (*pointing to another picture*) Who did the duck with the ice cream?
Wise Gold That was Moira.
Shepherd Oh, right. (*Nodding*) Her who smells of Marmite and can't have birthdays.
Wise Gold Ashley's not friends with me any more.

Shepherd (*waving a hand at the gallery*) Anyway, none of it really
'appened. My mum's got a farm an' she says they would never've ad'
oxes and asses in the same stall cos' they 'ave different bone meal.
Wise Gold Ashley ... isn't——
Shepherd Y'r a king, not a shepherd. Y' have t' stand with the kings.
Ass (*wandering off, addressing the world in general*) AM A DONKEY.

*Gabriel enters, killing Wise Gold with the worst look of all — not looking
at her*

Gabriel (*singing*) Away in a manger...
Wise Gold (*hopefully*) Hi?

*Angel enters. She finds this "ignoring her to death" more difficult and
gives Wise Gold a sad passing smile*

Ass (*quieter*) *Am* a donkey.

Ass wanders off, unnoticed, exiting via the boys' toilets

Wise Gold limps off, unloved, exiting via the girls' toilets

Narrator (*learning his lines with his eyes closed*) "And children came
from all over the world"

Gabriel starts combing her Jesus' hair again

Angel looks after where Wise Gold exited

Angel Do we ever talk to her again?
Gabriel Mmnope.

Never is a long time but the Angel has to accept it

Angel So did...? Is...? (*Thinking how to put it diplomatically*) Why are you
going to be Mary?
Gabriel (*snapping*) Prettiest is Mary.
Angel (*almost jumping*) Prettiest is.
Gabriel Is the rules. And who's prettiest out of me and Jenny Bennet?
Angel You are.
Gabriel I know.

Mary enters, as if on cue, having avoided the stick insect

Narrator (*finishing with a flourish*) It truly was — a silent night.

Herod OK. Ally McCoist, who is this? (*Falling to the floor in "slow motion", clutching his knee, apparently fouled, and then, still in slow motion, rolling around in agony mouthing terrible words and sticking the "V"s up*)

His new wife, Mary, puts a stop to this

Mary Right, so the Wise Man comes on——
Herod Geddoff.
Mary (*combing Herod's hair*) And he says "Have you 'ad a baby?" And you have to say "yes". And he says "what's his name?" And you say "Jesus". And y've got to look up. (*Raising Herod's head up*) You can't look down.
Herod Geddoff.

Herod bats his wife off and exits

Mary (*shouting after her husband*) And y've not combed y'r hair. Y've not... He's not combed his hair.
Gabriel (*to Mary, slyly*) You touched Ryan.
Mary (*slapping her hands on her sides in a very adult fashion*) Honestly, he'd go out without his trousers if they weren't on the chair.
Gabriel His step-brother had chickenpox.
Mary (*ignoring her and pointing*) And his crook! He's gone without his crook.
Gabriel The poxes are in your hand now.
Mary Honestly.
Gabriel In your hand, going up to y'r head, an' y'll sick up.
Mary (*leaving/escaping*) ⎱ (*together*) ⎰ Crook. Crook. Crook.
Gabriel (*shouting*) ⎰   ⎱ In a sock. Y'll sick in a sock an' y' won't be Mary. You're not gonna be Mary.

Mary escapes to the art wall where Shepherd is

Gabriel (*after a beat; quieter*) She's not gonna be Mary.
Angel No. You are.
Gabriel I am.
Narrator (*shuffling the cards to start again*) We were hoping to be in our new school hall.
Mary (*engineering a conversation at short notice*) So anyway so that's fine so who's him in the middle? Mary, Joseph...who's that fat man?
Shepherd John Burdgeon.
Mary Who?

Shepherd John. Who was there. Burdgeon. Who was there with Mary and Joseph. It says.

Mary Was 'e the one who dropped the baby off?

Shepherd Y' don't drop babies off. I saw one come out on the farm once. It comes out of your bum cover'd in yak.

Pause. Mary swallows audibly

Then this other thing comes out called a play centre an' that's like a pancake of blood. An' that lands on the floor, an' the dogs lick it and y'r mum kicks 'em. She says, "Go on, fly, bugger off."

Pause

Also y' moo a lot.

Mary Moo?

Shepherd Yeah.

Mary Like a cow?

Shepherd Yeah?

Mary Why?

Shepherd Cos it kills.

Gabriel (*combing Jesus; without turning*) So Jenny. *Still* want to be Mary?

Mary Yes.

Wise Gold and Star enter, arguing

Star Isn't. Isn't. Isn't.

Wise Gold It is. I'm just——

Star Isn't.

Wise Gold (*looking round; to Shepherd*) Zoe? When they have mince pies? Is it...when you leave mince pies for Father Christmas, who eats it? Is it Father Christmas or the Reindeer?

Innkeeper (*off, from his lair; calling*) MY DAD.

They all turn

The Innkeeper creaks opens the door of his lair, the Home Corner. Somehow he's got in there again. It's as if he has secret entrances to this place

Once again, that eerie music

Innkeeper A' seen 'im. In the living-room. All six mince pies. And the sherry.

The lair door creak-ks shut again. Everyone stands for a moment to ruminate on that piece of information

Suddenly the white teacher light appears, cueing huge clamour from everyone

Everyone (*variously*) Mizz Horrocks...!/Can I...?/He said.../Mizziz Horrocks...

This lasts for about two seconds, when the teacher light suddenly goes red accompanied by a tambourine slap

Everyone jabs fingers on lips. Silence

Under orders, the class shuffles into two clumps; boys (Narrator, Wise Frankincense and Star) on one side, and girls (Wise Gold, Shepherd, Mary, Angel and Gabriel) on the other

Looking up at the teacher light, Gabriel moves forwards

Gabriel (*sweetly*) Yes, Missis Horrocks.

They all watch the teacher light go off, at which point Gabriel snaps back to being Gabriel, only now with power

Toilets everyone. Boys go.

The boys shuffle off and exit to the boys' toilet

Girls go.

The girls shuffle off and exit to the girls' toilet

(*To Mary*) Not you, Jenny Bennet. You have to stay and tidy up.
Mary You're not monitor.
Gabriel (sotto voce, *spooking Mary out*) Wet, wet, wet.
Mary She just said "hold the door". That's not "toilet monitor".
Gabriel (*deadly; starting to follow the girls out*) "Hold the door" IS toilet monitor. Disobeyin' monitors IS naughty. Naughty DOES get you one sticker peeled off the "Who's Been Good?" Chart.

Gabriel smiles, evilly and spooks Mary again

Wet, wet, wet.
Mary (*bitterly, trumped*) Don't need to go.

Gabriel *Psssssssss.*
Mary Been already. Went before I came.

Pause

Gabriel starts to leave but comes back

Gabriel (*trying to psyche Mary out*) Don't wee y'r knickers, Jenny.

Gabriel exits

Mary doesn't want to get into trouble, so she can't disobey a monitor. She picks up the baby Jesus and starts to finish off any tidying up

Innkeeper draws a curtain in his lair and watches her

Innkeeper You know Aladdin?

Mary carries on tidying

Who we're seein' the panto of? In the panto? We're seein' the panto "Aladdin"?

Mary carries on tidying

That's where Jesus come from. (*This being his gold nugget of wisdom*) Out that lamp.

Mary carries on tidying

The Innkeeper emerges fully

My cousin saw it with cubs and when he rubs the lamp there's a big bang and glitter flies up which is on fire an' Aladdin drops the lamp and runs round holding his hand shouting: "Jesus Christ. Jesus Christ. Get Pauline". An' then the lights come on an' everyone has to go in the bar an' have a Fanta. You know Peter Crouch?

Mary carries on tidying

I picked him up.

Mary carries on tidying, unimpressed

An' once I picked up a great crested newt.

Mary does stop tidying at this, and turns

Innkeeper smells blood

   Great. Crested.
Mary Tiny.

Innkeeper shakes his head

Mary They're tiny. It was in assembly.
Innkeeper If it was tiny it wouldn't't've scared off the builders.

This is scaring the hell out of Mary

   It wouldn't't've stopped them building the hall.
Mary (*swallowing*) It's cause they're rare... it stops...
Innkeeper (*pointing outwards*) Big as that wall.
Mary (*swallowing again*) They're rare... and...
Innkeeper (*pointing to the back wall*) Big as that wall. And it can pick
   people up and go like that. (*He does a Japanese-movie "monster-eating-
   a-human" gesture*) Nggggyashyash.

Mary is clearly terrified, and as before, deals with it by avoiding it

Mary (*looking round*) And anyway tidy up, that's tidy, (*pointing*) *that's*
   tidy.

From off, the piano intro to Music 2. is heard

   (*Pointing "next door"*) And the juniors are doing the glockenspiels so
   it's us next.

Mary exits

Innkeeper (*desperately realizing he's losing his audience*) An' I picked it
   up. (*Hurriedly, calling*) I pick up loads. You could come round ours—
   (*swallowing*) ours and watch me pick stuff up.

But Mary's gone, leaving him at the door of the Home Corner

   (*Quieter*) At ours. (*His face falls into the expressionless shark-eyed glaze
   that makes him seem uncaring, impassive*)

Music 2. My House Always Smells of Beer

>   My house always smells of beer
>   My house smells of cigarettes
>   All the carpets smell of Stella

And the curtains, and my pets.
In the morning my dad showers
Scrubs himself for hours and hours
Sprays himself with body spray
Called "Lemon Zest for Active Men".
By the time I'm home from school
My dad'll smell of beer again.

Mary is firmly ushered back in by Gabriel from the girls' toilets

Gabriel (*to Mary*) Not clean. Clean it up. (*She makes something peripheral untidy*) Not clean. (*She goes, but darts back to spook Mary again*) Toilet. Toilet. *Pssssssswwsssss...*

Gabriel exits

On seeing Mary, Innkeeper achieves a greater degree of lyricism

Innkeeper   Jenny Bennet smells of summer
Jenny Bennet smells of flowers
Like the ones outside the
Caravan in Conway, next to ours.
If I stand by Jenny Bennet
In the queue for dinner,
Then it feels like I have found the spell
To an Aladdin's lamp of smell.
If she gave my clothes a rub
All she would smell is our pub.

Innkeeper exits

Narrator, Mary, Wise Gold and Shepherd enter

There is a huge kerfuffle

Narrator Starting! They're coming in. Get your stuff!
Wise Gold "Stuff"!
Shepherd "Little Town of Bethlehem". Get your stuff.

Wise Frankincense enters to get his plastic bottle wrapped in crepe paper

Wise Frankincense Everyone get their thtuff. Get the myrrh.
Wise Gold (*off hand to the new kid*) Adrian, you're not doin' myrrh now. Darren's got chickenpox, and I can't go straight back after doing the gold, so now I'm (*swapping with him*) — doing the myrrh an' you're doing frankincense. Hey! (*To Mary*) Seen what I've got for Jesus?

Wise Frankincense (*his world collapsing*) Frankinthenth?
Wise Gold (*producing an All Gold box of chocolates*) "All Gold". Solid
— gold. Present off me mum. And-d... (*producing an ornate, plastic, container*) this off me mum an' all.
Mary What is it?
Wise Gold (*reading*) "Bath salts to combat stress". (*Pause*) Does your mum not give you these?
Wise Frankincense (*swallowing*) Actually d'you want to thwap?
Shepherd Does she want to "what"?
Wise Frankincense Prethenth.
Shepherd *What*?
Wise Frankincense For Jethuth.
Shepherd For *who*?
Wise Gold There has to be a gap. I do gold, you do frankincense, I go back an' do myrrh.
Shepherd (*pointing at Wise Frankinsence, off hand*) Doesn't he sound like him in the donkey 'ead? You sound like one of the special unit kids.
Wise Frankincense Get lotht.
Shepherd (*frowning*) Get *what*?

Gabriel enters with Angel, who is carrying Gabriel's doll, in tow

Gabriel (*nods and points; to Angel*) OK sit there.

Angel sits

OK say it.
Angel (*praying*)   Gentle Jesus meek and mild
                        Look upon a little child
                        But please don't look on Jenny Bennet
                        And give her chicken pox.
Gabriel (*nodding*) Right. Now give it her.
Angel Jenny?

Angel dutifully holds up Gabriel's doll like an auctioneer's assistant

Mary That's not Jesus.
Angel (*turning to Gabriel*) She says that's not Jesus.
Gabriel That *is* Jesus. In the book.
Mary There he is-s! (*She pulls out her Jesus, the one with the oversized head and goon-y grin*)
Angel Awwww!
Gabriel In the book-k! (*To support her argument, Gabriel presents a ripped-out piece of an illustrated bible*) In the book, in the book-k. He's got blonde hair an' a proper face hasn't he, Shamima?

Angel (*to Mary's doll*) Kookoo!

Bad move. Gabriel looks at Angel with steely death

Gabriel (*casually*) Jess?

Wise Gold is immediately at her side

Wise Gold Yes?
Angel (*sensing what's coming and leaping in to avoid disaster*) No...no...
Gabriel Let's not talk to Shamima.

    Gabriel walks off and exits with Wise Gold following obediently

Angel is horror-stricken

The white teacher light appears

Mary Everyone ready!

    Everyone exits except Shepherd

Shepherd Miss Horrocks? (*He points to the Home Corner*) Bradley's still
in the Home Corner, Mizz Horrocks, 'cause of getting busted... (*She goes
to the Home Corner*) 'Cause of not doing what he was told. 'Cause he
never does 'cause he was born fifteen minutes after me, but me mum's
sure he's got a different dad 'cause I'm all right but he turned out a right
sod and that's why he wrote "I have" on his "Who's Been Good" chart an'
(*pointing*) that's why he's in here, 'cause of never doin' what you tell him.
(*She looks in the Home Corner*) He's not here, Miss Horrocks.

Dark music of evil a-doing. Black-out

SCENE 2

Mrs Horrocks' Special Place

*Inside Mrs Horrocks' special place is Innkeeper, like Norman Bates,
peering into the darkness. He is not fazed by being in forbidden places.
Cr-r-reak. The door into this sacred, forbidden cupboard swings open*

Star (*off*) Peter-r. Peter Crou-uch? Peter ... *Bradley*!

Star enters, markedly less confident about being in forbidden places. He sees Innkeeper in there, and jumps

Innkeeper hardly reacts

I had him in me hand, I was holding him and what he—just he—what made me drop him was he jumped.

Innkeeper stares into the darkness. Star almost dare not peer in

S'not allowed in there. Store cupboard's Mrs Horrocks' special place.
Innkeeper (*pausing, then deadly low*) Dares y'.
Star There's darker places than that. In the NASA space centre at Uncle Ted's. So they all get used to bein' —all get used...
Innkeeper Dares y'.
Star (*steering away at high speed*) Your dad can't be Santa Claus 'cause you wouldn't be Bradley Jerrams you'd be Bradley Claus hey I got something you haven't. (*He "wobbles" one of his front teeth*) See that? That means it'll come out, and that... (*leaning in*) y'get *money.*

Innkeeper looks at Star, killing him with silence. He bids him enter

The piano introduction to Music 3. starts underscore

Star (*sensing a way out*) Ah, that's...! Ah, what a... (*pointing*) ah, I would go in, but we have to be back now, singing.

Innkeeper kills him softly with his look

I would but that's "Bethlehem". We have to be back there now, singing.
Innkeeper (*leaning in*) Big Gay Girl.
Star (*calling*) We have to be stood back there.

The Innkeeper exits

(*Calling limply after him*) We have to be stood back there.

Music 3. Don't Grow Up Like Your Dad

Everyone else (*off*) O little town of Bethlehem
Star (*limply, to no-one in particular*) We have to be stood back there.
Everyone else (*off*) Beneath thy deep...
Star (*to himself*) But that'll mean that Bradley
                            Thinks that I did not dare.

And I dare! I absolutely d— anyway my dad,
He (*mimicking dad's gesture*) whorr, he says,
He whorr — he says
"You're like me, son,
We're good as anyone".
So (*gesturing*) Bradley! Just (*gestures*) you.

Star slams the door. The music actually stops as if that's that. Then the door creaks open again

Everyone else (*off; singing*) How silently...
Star   But that'll mean that Bradley
                                       Thinks that I did not dare.
Everyone else (*off; singing*) So God imparts
Star   And grown ups have to start to
                                       Do things that make 'em scared.
                                       Like my mum once told my dad to
                                       "Don't dare talk about my friend like that."
                                       And he did! He dared!
                                       I heard him on the stairs,
                                       He called Uncle Ted a "*Prat*".

                                       He said he didn't like it
                                       Having Uncle
                                       Ted spending time with me.
                                       'Cause Ted thinks that he's
                                       God because he went to
                                       Hope university.
                                       And he uses words my dad has
                                       Only ever heard of
                                       In the House of Lords, and
                                       Buys big presents
                                       Just to make the point my
                                       Dad only works at Ford's.

                                       And then Mum cries
                                       And makes me promise I
                                       Won't grow up like my dad.
                                       But Dad says "Son, you're gonna be like me."
                                       So that's gonna make him sad.
Everyone else (*off; singing*) We hear the heavenly...
Star (*gritting his teeth*) I'm going to do it, Bradley!
Everyone else (*off; singing*) Great glad tidings tell...

Star stands in the room like a kid daring a very cold sea

Star (*stepping in*) Ohh hell
               HE'S THERE. HE'S THERE. I'm
               Like my dad, I dared.
Star ⎫ (*together*) ⎰ Now I am a man as well.
Everyone else (*off*) ⎭   ⎱ Our Lord Emanuel.

Black-out

The Lights immediately up on

SCENE 3

The wings

Over the stage there have been some curtains hastily hung up either side, effectively forming the "wings"; L (the girls' toilet exit) are the girls' wings. R (the boys' toilet exit) are the boys' wings

Narrator enters without cards, like a trapeze artist with no net

Angel enters behind him

Angel Is your mum here?
Narrator (*stopping her*) Don't. Y'r not allowed to look through.
Angel (*in a reflex*) Don't wannoo.
Narrator (*pointing "across the stage"*) You have to stay where they can't see y' 'til Mizz Horrocks nods.
Angel (*in a girl versus boy reflex*) Smell of you now, y' nugget.

Wise Gold enters behind them

Angel (*to Wise Gold*) Smell of him now. (*Desperate to try and engage Wise Gold in forbidden discourse*) D'you want to play pretend?
Narrator Y'*can't*. Y' have to wait for the nod-d.

Even Wise Gold realizes this is a rather strange time to be playing pretend

Wise Gold Ashley won't let me-e.
Narrator (*peering for his "cue"*) Shhh.
Angel All right. Let's play breakfasts. You be dad. And let's pretend you

say "I'm going to work". We're playing breakfasts. "I'm going to the
workshop, I need breakfast, don't I? I can't go out to work without
nothing in me can I? And I want white sandwiches." Right you've said
that. (*Perfunctorily "ironing" something*) Right and now you're come
back from work and you've come back and I say "Umran's been fighting
with that Vorbani kid in Kwik-Save again" and you say——

Wise Gold Why?

Angel 'Cause of them being from India and us bein' from Pakistan. And
you say——

Wise Gold "Go to your room".

Angel No no, you say "Well done, lad. Don't let anyone call you a coon,
'specially not a little coon like him', and then——

Wise Gold What's a coon?

Angel (*trying to stay with the game*) I don't know. An' then you go to
sleep. That can be the bedroom.

Narrator My dad doesn't sleep in the bedroom.

Angel and Wise Gold look at him

He used to sleep in the bedroom. Then he slept on the settee. Now he
doesn't sleep at our house at all.

Angel and Wise Gold look at him

He's coming tonight, though. I've learnt me words.

Angel My mum's comin' but she doesn't see much, cos she always has to
make sure she's got her back to Mrs Vorbani.

Wise Gold Why?

Angel Is yours?

Wise Gold She does other things, my mum.

Angel Does she?

Wise Gold Oh yeah.

Angel Like what?

Wise Gold (*cheerfully*) Bingo.

Narrator (*nodding*) Th— NOD! "GO"!

SCENE 4

The stage

The stage lights come up on Narrator

Narrator (*loudly and proudly*) Ladies and gentlemen. Welcome to

Flint Street Junior School and our nativity. We are in Mrs Horrocks' classroom again this year because the builders diggin' for the new school hall found some great crested newts which meant they have to er... they er... (*he tries to remember, goes to look, but doesn't let himself*) ...well, they go off an' do that new Asda.

In the girls' wings, Mary drags up Herod and has a final check

Mary Don't look at your mum an' dad.
Herod (*batting her off*) I'm not.
Mary Look up, but not at your mum and dad.
Herod I'm not gonna look at me dad, all right?
Narrator In Nazareth lived Mary and Joseph.

Herod walks on. He immediately looks at his mum and dad

Herod (*with a creeping smile*) There's me dad.
Mary (sotto voce) *Don't.*

Herod manages a surreptitious wave to his dad, from under his cloak

Narrator Joseph was a carpenter.

Very bossily Mary sits and positions Herod next to her

Mary Joseph stands there.
Narrator One day Joseph was at work.
Mary Right, Joseph goes off.

Herod exits, looking a bit "well what the hell was all that for then"?

Narrator Mary was on her own at home.
Mary (*getting up and miming hoovering;* sotto voce) There we go. Never stops does it. Ha. Dress like a tart. You want me to dress like a tart?
Narrator Suddenly there was a beautiful light which filled the room.

Gabriel walks up through the wings and enters, her hands held limply in the air, her eyes cold with hatred

Gabriel Eh.
Mary (*turning and standing her ground*) What?

It's starting to feel more like a spaghetti western than a nativity

Gabriel (*dripping with death*) I bring wonderful news of great joy.
Mary (*to herself and Gabriel*) Know what it is.
Gabriel You're gonna 'ave a baby and it's God's an' it's gonna be called Jesus.
Mary Knew that already.
Gabriel (*gritting her teeth she moves in;* sotto voce, *just for Mary*) An' it's gonna have blonde hair.

Gabriel storms off, striking Mary with her wings without realizing, and exits through the girls' exit

Mary goes off to the boys' wings, glaring back

Narrator Ceasar Ugustus made a degree that everyone had to go home and pay for taxis.

In the boys' wings Innkeeper is relishing standing by Mary. He breathes in her smell deeply

Mary (*a bit narked*) will y' stop smellin' me?

Innkeeper skulks off out through the boys' exit

On the stage

Narrator So Mary and Joseph had to start out on a long journey.

In the boys' wings

Mary (*urgently whispering to Herod*) Donkey. An' don't look.

Herod enters

Mary and Herod drag Pedro – the Spanish donkey on wheels — on to the stage

How far is it to Bethlehem?

Herod immediately looks at his mum and dad with a wry smile

(*Prompting Herod from the side of her mouth*) "A long way."

Herod is still looking at his mum and dad with a wry smile

(*Still prompting Herod*) He says "A long way, Mary, but you can ride on the donkey". (*She gives up and looks at the Narrator to say "carry on";* sotto voce) He's said it.

Narrator On the journey, Mary thought——

Mary (sotto voce) He goes off now. (*She nudges Herod off*)

Herod exits

Narrator ——Mary thought about what the Angel had said about her baby. (*Trying to remember*) And God. (*Was that right?*) It being God's. (*That'll do*) And that.

The piano introduction to Music 4. starts

Gabriel enters

What follows is a duet of an Angel and a Virgin without much sense of peace or innocence. Mary sings the words all the way through. Gabriel's mind wanders

Music 4. A Way To Kill Mary

Mary Away in a manger	**Gabriel** A way to kill Mary
No crib for a bed,	No crib for a bed,
The little Lord Jesus	I could take her to the water tray
Laid down his sweet head.	And hold down her sweet head.
The stars in the bright sky	The stars insects lots of crawly insects
Look down where he lay,	All shoved every where he lay,
The little Lord Jesus	The little cow can't stand any
Asleep on the hay.	Crawly creeps on the hay.
The cattle are lowing	My mum bought me a bible book
The poor baby wakes,	At the school car boot sale.
But the little Lord Jesus	No-one looks like (*pointing at Mary*) her, except
No crying he makes.	For Noah's wife and Jonah's whale.
I love thee Lord Jesus	She's only Mary 'cause she knows it all,
Look down from the sky,	An' goes (*mimicking Mary*) look down from the sky.
And stay by my cradle	An' her school jumper has not
Till morning is nigh.	Got holes in like mine.

Mary gets a recorder out to play the melody

Gabriel does an immediate eyes to heaven

Gabriel Oh and yes of *course* she plays recorder, obviously.
She does that, for God's sake!
And her mum made her a little case for her recorder
Shaped like a snake.
My mum blew mine in a barbecue to get the
Fire going one day
Now it's black at the bottom end
And is shaped like a "J".

(*Speaking*) But it's not fair, see it's not *fair.*

Mary la, la's the melody and dances

(*Singing*) I did not bite holes in my school jumper.
That was my sister
Who is not my sister anyway.
She's taller and her hair's a diff'rent colour
And *her* mum's called Kay
But I always have to have her clothes when she's been in them first
And that's just not fair,
But my mum said:
"Sister, right she is your sister, even
If she's half a one now get upstairs".

Mary Be near me Lord Jesus	**Gabriel** Last year Dad bought a
I ask thee to stay,	"Mary" dress
Close by me forever	For my sister to wear,
And love me I pray!	This year I said, "Miss, I've got
Bless all the dear children	The Mary dress it's hanging there"
In thy tender care,	She said our family'd done it once
And fit us for heaven	So it wouldn't be fair,
To live with thee there.	And fit us for heaven
	To live with thee there.

Gabriel exits via the the girls' wings. Innkeeper enters via the boys' wings

Mary goes to exit via the boys' wings, where she is stopped by Innkeeper

Mary What?

Innkeeper hands Mary a tooth

What is it?

Innkeeper, robbed of speech in her company, can't say anything

Is it a bit of polo?

Shepherd enters

Shepherd (*casually factual as ever*) If anyone wants to see some blood, the Star of Bethlehem's spittin' in the sink 'cause his front tooth's come out.

Mary looks at what's in her hand and drops it on reflex

Mary Ee-urgh.
Innkeeper (*pointing forlornly at the tooth*) Y' get money for it.

Mary walks away

(*Calling after Mary*) Y' get money.

Mary exits

Innkeeper and Shepherd watch Mary go. Shepherd nods like an old man at the bar of a rural pub

Shepherd You love 'er.

Pause. Innkeeper keeps looking where Mary went

Innkeeper Bog off.
Shepherd Y' love her an' y' want to marry 'er.
Innkeeper Bog off.
Shepherd Y'wanna make y'r hair nice.

Innkeeper gets down to look for his dental "metaphorical" engagement ring

Her dad, when they got married, there's photos everywhere. (*Indicating hair*) Totally tidy.

Innkeeper finds the tooth and stands

Auntie Debbie. When she got married, when I was bridesmaid and you were pageboy an' had pyjamas under your trousers 'cause they pricked, that Ross, who she married, *he* had neat hair.
Innkeeper (*looking at all he has in the world to offer; grudgingly*) What else d'y have?

Shepherd Big tent. Y' should have a big tent for the disco after, but there
in't any money 'cause the government've give it all to the French sods so
you have to have it in a scout hut.

Pause

Innkeeper (q*uieter, on auto pilot*) Bog off.
Shepherd That's what happens. You make your hair nice if y' love
someone. That's why she's always combin' Ryan's. (*Beat*) Bet she loves Ryan.

SCENE 5

*The scene opens with Ryan, aka Herod, singing his ("A Question of Sport")
theme tune*

Herod Dah digga dah dum do dum...

*Music as sections of the playground apparatus appear. (The top of this is
what we could see through the rear classroom window)*

Ok now. Ally McCoist. Which of these was not in the nineteen ninety-six
Canadian bobsleigh team? (*In a different voice*) Oh come on, don't do
it to me, Sue. Don't do it to me.

Mary enters, having tracked down her errant husband

The piano introduction to Music 5 starts inside

Mary Get down! Get... We're not allowed in the playground. We're not
allowed on apparatus without a dinner lady.
Herod (*annoyed at being found*) Don't.
Mary (*over the music*) We have to help with the singing!
Herod (*pointing at Mary*) Don't comb me hair.
Mary Even if we're not on the stage. Miss Horrocks said we have to sing
wherever we are. That's why you learn—that's why y'r mum does them
with you. Did your mum an' dad learn the words with you?
Herod (*after a pause*) Yeah.
Mary (*firmly*) Well y' have to do what y' did with your mum an' dad,
then.

Music 5. Watch How Mummy Does It

*From Mary and Herod we get the full story. From inside (off), we hear
whatever shrapnel of the lyric has been recalled by everyone else*

Mary   **Everyone else** (sotto voce; *off*)
  Once in royal David's city   Once in royal David's city
  Stood a lowly cattle shed.   Stood a lowly cattle shed.
  That's not bad,
  Now watch how mummy does it,
  (*very pronounced*) Een a may-nger forrr hees bed.
  People need to hear each word you say
  If you're chairman of the P.T.A.

Herod   **Everyone else** (*off*)
  Once in royal David, hold on   Once in royal David...
  Sorry mate, just let me take this call.
  Hallo? No. We're only learning carols.
  No, you're interrupting nothing, Paul.
  That last statement ... oh, would you believe.
  I've a call now coming in from Steve.

Mary   **Herod**
  Stand up straight

                               Just sit on that settee, mate
  Watch my lips

                               And watch some dvds mate,
  (*head down*) Don't look down.

                               Have you found the one you
  (*head up*) Like that!   like? That
                               funny sport quiz on the BBC?

  (Just practice) 't's. T - t "try saying
  post-nativity-hospitality".

                               Hallo?
  Jenny?

                               Steven?
  Ready?

                               Bollocks. You still there?
  And *go*!

                               I don't know the carols
  Come on! 'car-rols!' roll those 'r's

                               But I know who won the R-r-ryder
                               cup.
  (Like mummy) "R-red wine
  for the r-raffle"

                               And the last Australian open
  Open wide and don't look down

                               Down hill slalom, and gymnastics.

Stick your chest out
And your head up!
And I'll be with you,
When you do it in the hall.

                              And he'll be with me....
                              When he's made that one last call.

Scene 6

The boys' and girls' wings

A piano interlude finishing the last number continues a short while

The Lights come up to reveal Angel and Wise Gold in one wing, waiting

Angel Is Bradley's dad really Santa Claus?

The Lights come up to reveal Innkeeper standing forlornly in the opposite wing

My dad's just an electrician. (*Beat*) Mister Vorbani mends cars. His brothers are always scrapping with my brothers. My mum says Mrs Vorbani showed off at Easter when her Pakra was in Joseph's Dreamcoat, an' she made special hot cross buns with Jesus's face on and Mister Vorbani made him a magic coat with millions of car paints from his garage.

Wise Gold Like Jesus?

Angel Mister Vorbani? He's not like Jesus. My dad says he's like what Noel Edmonds'd be like if he was Indian.

Wise Gold No, but wasn't Jesus a car painter?

Gabriel (*to Angel; off*) Was she talking to you?

Wise Gold and Angel swing round on a pin

   Gabriel enters like Mrs Danvers from the toilets

Wise Gold shakes her head, but the game's up

Wise Gold No. No, I wasn't—we were just—she was...

Gabriel Right. Shamima. (*Swooping off*) Let's not talk to Jess.

   Gabriel exits

There's a moment where Angel smiles apologetically at Wise Gold like friends condemned to separation. But she has to obey

Wise Gold exits after Gabriel and gets into position behind the door on the stage

Scene 7

The stage

Narrator walks back on

Narrator Bethlehem was very busy with people payin' for taxis. Mary and Joseph tried to find somewhere to stay the night.

Mary and Herod emerge on to the stage, and go to the door

Herod, plus donkey, just looks out every time he's on stage, as though he's been stunned by some electrical pads

Mary (*loudly*) We are very tired and my wife is having a baby. Have you any room?
Wise Gold (*opening the door in tears, shaking her head*) there—is— no—room. (*She shuts the door*)
Narrator Mary and Joseph went to try at another inn.

Mary leads Herod in a rough circle around the stage, in order to return to the same door. All the time Herod is looking at his dad

This time, Star opens the door, with his star on his head. They look at him a beat. The door shuts

A moment later, Star opens the door with the star not on his head

Mary (*loudly*) My wife is tired and having a baby. Is there any room?
Star "Is there any room"? "Do we have a room"? Now then. Let me think. Let's have a look at the book... (*He goes inside the door and mimes "looking at a book"*) "room-room-room". One sec. (*He shuts the door*)

Mary and Herod wait patiently

Innkeeper, watching Mary from the boys' wings, feels his sticky-up hair. Shepherd is at his shoulder

Shepherd You watch. If she tidies his hair. If she tidies his hair, that's what it means.

The waiting Mary looks at Herod. She can't resist ...

She's gonna do it-t ...

Mary touch-tidies Herod's hair

That's it. (*He slaps Innkeeper on the back*) Sorry, mate. She loves Ryan.

Shepherd exits

Star enters the girls' wings

Star (*getting really into this "looking" acting*) "Is there a room"? Dum dum... (*checking for availability*) nope. Uncle Ted's in that on-ne. (*Checking another*) Nope, Buzz Aldrin's in that—— (*finger to lips, caught in the red glare*) Sorry, Missis Horrocks.

There is the bang bang bang of footsteps and Star reappears at the door on stage, rather hurriedly

No. (*He shuts the door abruptly*)

Mary and Herod walk round in a circle again, to get to the same door

Narrator Mary and Joseph had almost given up hope. Finally they came to one very last inn. It was all on its own at the very edge of the town. They knocked on the door.

Mary knocks on the door

Inside this inn, they found a very *friendly* Innkeeper.

Deathly horror music. The door opens like that of the Bates motel. Behind it, from the darkness appears the dead-eyed face of Innkeeper, he is truly chilling

Mary We...argh. (*Slightly put on the back foot; swallowing*) We are tired and having a baby. Is there a room in the...

Innkeeper looks at Mary

...inn?

Innkeeper slowly turns to Herod, who takes some degree of cover, then back at Mary. He breathes in to speak, points at Mary, prepares the first word

Innkeeper You...

Upon which, there is a huge horror-movie music sting

BLACK-OUT

ACT II

Scene 1

The stage

We return to almost the exact point we left off, with a slight recap

Narrator Mary and Joseph had almost given up hope. Finally they came to one very last inn. It was all on its own at the very edge of the town. They knocked on the door.

Mary knocks

Inside this inn, they found a very friendly Innkeeper.

The door opens like that of the Bates' motel. Behind it, from the darkness appears the dead-eyed face of Innkeeper, he is truly chilling

Mary We...*argh*. (*Slightly put on the back foot; swallowing*) We are tired and having a baby.

Innkeeper looks at Mary

Is there a room in the inn?

Innkeeper looks at Herod, then back at Mary. Pause

Innkeeper You can come in. (*He nods at Herod*) But he can bugger off.

There is a simultaneous flurry of activity as the red teacher light flares on, the piano thunders in playing an impromptu recap of Once in Royal, and Innkeeper disappears through the door backwards, slamming it as he goes

Narrator Ther-at night, in ... (*He stops dead as he shouldn't be talking yet*)

Ass enters from the boys' wings, carrying a haybale and the doll concealed behind it

Ass (*always shouting*) HAYBALE, HAYBALE, HAYBALE ...

Mary ends up on the haybale, Herod beside her with Pedro the lascivious donkey, and Ass

The piano stops

Narrator That night, in the cold bare stable, Mary gave birth to a little baby.
Mary (*bringing out her goony-faced doll from behind the haybale; quietly*) Moo. M-mm-ooo. (*She rocks it*)

The piano plays a few desultory bars of "Baby Jesus Do Not Stir", underscore

Narrator (*over the music; nudging Ass*) That's my mum!

Ass looks out, not that you can really tell where he's looking. After a few seconds of lullaby, he nudges Narrator back and points

Ass (*loudly, muffled*) THAT'S MY SOCIAL WORKER.

Shepherd is in the wings, waiting for her cue. She notices the rejected Wise Gold at her side

The lullaby continues underscore

Wise Gold Is it you, now? Are you doin' it now? When we go to see *Aladdin* d'you want to sit next to me on the bus?

Slight pause

Shepherd What?
Wise Gold It's a nice sheep, that. Can I come to your farm? Have you got any sheep like this?
Shepherd (*looking at the the rather odd sheep-toy she's been given*) Not like this.
Wise Gold Have you got Shepherds?
Shepherd Our Shepherd comes from eastern Europe and he wouldn't shave his beard off 'cause of his church and me mum said, "sod his church, he'll get sheep ticks" and he wouldn't, and he got a sheep tick that filled up with yeller and burst in Asda.

The beautiful lullaby stops

Mary goes to the boys' wings where she waits

Ass and Herod exit through the girls' wings

Narrator In the fields round Bethlehem there were some Shepherds.

Shepherd walks on and sits with her sheep, leaving Wise Gold slightly reeling from that last image.

As they sat watching their flocks...

Shepherd looks, studiedly, at the sheep under her arm

Narrator ... there was a bright light in the sky above them.

Gabriel enters from one side, Angel trails on after her

Some Angels app——
Gabriel (*on one-note, like Reuters*) Jesus. Born in Bethlehem. Lord. Lying in a manger.

Gabriel goes to the other side, the boys' wings, followed by Angel

Narrator (*having to finish*) ...some Angels appeared.

In the wings, Gabriel runs into Mary with her baby Jesus

Gabriel (*still on one-note*) Jesus. Stupid face. Lyin' in a sink. (*She seizes Jesus from Mary and chucks it into the toilets*)
Mary (*racing after it*) Ashley-y!

Mary exits

Narrator It was very shiny and filled the three Shepherds with wonder.

Narrator exits through the girls' wings

Music 6. Shiny Silver Caravan

Shepherd   } While Shepherds watched their flocks by night
Everyone else (*off*) } All seated on the ground,
Shepherd They wouldn't have three Shepherds,
        'Cause sheep only cost eight pound.

The only shiny thing that turned up
In our fields at night
Was this amazing caravan
All silvery and white.

My dad, he saw and shouted out
The word that makes mum cross,
He said he'd have to shift them, 'cause the
Cops won't give a toss.

My mum said we should all be nice to travellers
At Christmas, and relax,
My dad said it was - not the same 'cause Joseph had a
Job and paid some tax.

He stuck his pitchfork through the tyres of the caravan,
And called them "sponging louts",
While we were getting screwed by all the supermarkets
On the price of sprouts.

And then the sky was full of weird noises
And the word that makes mum cross,
The man inside the caravan
Put tents up for the
Circus, and was lost.

Everyone else (*off*) Mrr mrr gll nrr
Shepherd My dad was very angry,
Everyone else (*off*) Nee nur la
Shepherd He gave the judge a sign.
Everyone else (*off*) Bllr nerr nee naa
Shepherd And now he drives a taxi cab
              At night to pay the fine.

              So on our farm we think that (*counting*) cops and
Travellers and circus men
And judges "All deserve a bloody
pitchfork up the crease".
Everyone Good will henceforth from heaven to men
              begin and never cease.

Shepherd (*speaking*) Thank you.

SCENE 2

Mrs Horrocks' Special Place

Innkeeper is in there, just a shape in the darkness; there is tense music

Star opens the door to it. He has a tube of glue

Star Peter-r? (*Peering round*) Peter Crouch-h?

The door opens shedding light on Innkeeper

Star (*jumping*) N-ya ha. (*He covers it with a swagger, remembering he's a man now*) I been in here. I come in here a lot now. I'm gluing the floor in case Peter Crouch come b... (*remembering something else*) ...you said "bugger off".

The Innkeeper looks at him, dead eyed

Mizz Horrocks's gone mad. She's gonna tell y'r dad.
Innkeeper It's me dad who says it. S'what you say. Big John and Big John's dad who do our door on Fridays, if they don't want someone to come in, they say, "You can come in pet but your monkey can bugger off".

Star swallows

Then if the bloke tries to climb in through the gents' window, they take him round the back an' push a bottle skip into his testicles.
Star Right.

Innkeeper clicks his fingers for the glue. Star tries to ignore it

She says she's gonna have to put the overhead projector on. An' she didn't want to do that.

Innkeeper clicks his fingers again for the glue

'Cause it'd be all right if we had the new hall, but in here it's too bright an' everyone gets an 'eadache.

Innkeeper clicks his fingers again for the glue

Star, reluctant to relinquish it, looks at it

Hey. "Stick" insect! (*Pointing to the glue*) "Stuck"!

Innkeeper doesn't smile

Star finally surrenders the glue, attempting not to feel pressured into it

Yeah I er—think I'll let you borrow it.

Innkeeper nods for Star to go

Yeah, I think I might decide to go now.

Star exits

Innkeeper looks at the glue. We feel a plot is hatching. He holds it up and squeezes some into his hand from a height

There is music of doom

SCENE 3

The Stage

Ass is standing next to his haybale

Narrator enters

Narrator (*getting quite confident now, hardly looking at his cards*) The Shepherds came down from the hills to find the stable.

Mary and Herod enter from one side; Herod is pulling the donkey, Mary has the baby Jesus doll

They wanted to see if what the Angel had told them was true. When they walked in, they were filled with peace. The night outside was cold and starry. But in here, everything was golden, sweet from the smell of the hay and warm from the gentle breath of the animals.

Shepherd enters from the opposite side

Mary sits down on the haybale. Ass nods nearby

Shepherd An Angel told us——
Ass (*seemingly in some distress, jigging one leg*) —MISS 'ORROCKS?
Shepherd An Angel told us——

Ass —MISS 'ORROCKS?

Mary (*narked at this disruption of a beautiful moment*) Shhh-t.

Ass NEED THE TOILET. COULDN'T GO AT THE START. (*Pointing to his snout*) COULDN'T GET NEAR THE TROUGH, 'CAUSE OF ME HEAD.

Shepherd (*in a very loud, flat monotone*) An Angel told us there was a baby in this barn is it true.

Mary (*smiling angelically*) Yes! (*Proudly holding the baby Jesus up for Shepherd to see, head up, shoulders back, very clear*) His name is Jesus, and he has come to save mankind.

Jesus' head falls off quite heavily on to the floor with a thud, everyone looks at it

Shepherd (*casual as ever*) Jesus head's fell off.

Mary (*shouting off*) That's *your fault, Ashley,* throwin' it in the sink.

Ass (*putting his hand up*) I'VE WET ME LEG.

Pedro, the toy donkey pulled by Herod, collapses to the floor

Pedro (*voiced by someone else*) Clip clop. Clip clop. Clip clop.

Shepherd Get him off before he swears.

Pedro (*making a rather lascivious noise*) Eh, *señorita*! Nice ass.

Shepherd Too late.

Black-out

SCENE 4

The playground

It is dark, there is strange music and a strange noise

Wise Frankincense is sitting on the playground equipment, far too high up for his own safety, with the look of a regal suicide bid

Wise Frankincense   (*making a sound like a big bee or a wasp*) Szz... eeeezzzz... Szzz-uzzeeeeezzzzz... (*Taking a vocal run-up*) She zzells zzzzea shells. (*He winces*) And thaxaphone-th. And thaxaphone-th. (*He pauses*) She zzells zzzzea shells on the... (*He stops, looks down*)

Ass enters below, with his right foot in a Co-op bag. He takes his time before speaking

Ass (*pointing; shouting*) NOT ALLOWED ON THAT WITHOUT A DINNER LADY.

The music of strangeness stops

Wise Frankincense doesn't respond

(*Indicating his ass's head*) GOOD, THIS, INNIT? I'M KEEPING IT ON F'REVER. S'BETTER THAN MY REAL 'EAD.

Wise Frankincense still doesn't doesn't respond. He isn't receiving visitors

Ass, not really caring much, sits on the bottom rung of the frame and looks at his right foot

(*Pointing to his foot*) THEY LIVE IN SWIMMING POOLS, VERUCCAS.

Wise Frankincense doesn't respond

(*Looking up again*) Y'LL BE LIKE THAT BOY IN MAGHULL. Y'LL FALL OFF AN' Y'R LEG BONE COMES OUT OF Y'R BUM. (*Adding a bit of another story*) DOGS LICK IT. (*Pause*) DIDN'T DIE, THOUGH. (*Pause*) MY GRAN DIED. (*He sniffs*) SHE WAS OLD. WHAT DAD SAID. BUT SHE WASN'T. COS I LOOKED IN THE BACK OF HER CARDIGAN ONCE AN' SHE WAS ONLY 38 TO 40. (*Pointing "inside"*) DON'T Y' WAN'T T'BE IN IT? (*It is troubling him that Wise Frankincense is up there*)
Wise Frankincense I don't want t' thay what I've brought.

Pause

Ass WHY, IS IT SHIT?

Wise Frankincense finally looks down. He can't suppress a slight smile of horror on hearing this word

Wise Frankincense You can't say that.

Ass looks up

(*Beat*) It's one of the wordth that'th forbidden. "shit" ith. (*Beat*) Like "prithon".
Ass (*looking up*) WE SAY "PRISON".

Wise Frankincense shakes his head. He can't

WHAT D'YOU SAY?
Wise Frankincense "Daddy'th working in the Far Eath-t".
Ass (*nodding; looks back*) WE SAY IT WHEN WE SEE ME MUM.
Wise Frankincense (*suddenly energized*) Is she in prithon? What did she do? Did she wash lot-th of money for th-ome people in Gibraltar?
Ass NO, SHE STOLE JEANS FROM MATALAN.

Music 7. starts quietly; off

(*Pointing*) "DING DONG"! BEST ONE, "DING DONG". DID THEY HAVE THAT WHERE YOU USED TO COME FROM?

Wise Frankincense doesn't respond

Ass climbs up to nudge Wise Frankincense's leg

WHAT'S THE MATTER?
Wise Frankincense (*blurting it out*) I have to practise "th-ea shellth". Otherwise I sound like one of the kidth in the thpecial unit.

Pause

Ass I'M IN THE SPECIAL UNIT.

Wise Frankincense looks down

Y'GET A LONGER PLAYTIME AND BISCUITS.
Wise Frankincense I can't thay "frankinthenth".
Ass Y'CAN SAY "SHIT". (*Shrugging*) SAY "FRANKINSHIT".

Music 7. If There Was A God

Wise Frankincense (*singing along randomly ad-libbed with the intro*)
          Ding dong, ding dong, ding (*etc*)

          If there was a God at all
          There would be no Jethuth.
          There would be a Johnothan
          Or Craig or Anthony not a Jethuth.
          Arnold. David. There are loads of names without an "S"
          Why did he pick "Jethuth"?

Ass   When you're in a donkey's head
You can say "bum" and "willy".
When you're in a donkey's head
They don't know if you've carried on too LONG,
Or sang on one note all the time,
Or (*sticking his tongue out*) stuck your tongue out,
Or gone "Boobs, boobs, boobs like Jordan"
I love bein' a donkey.
Sausages.
Bum,
Fart,
Crap, bum,
Willy is what you can say
When Miss thinks you're a donkey.

Wise Frankincense	**Everyone else** (*off*)
If you don't thpeak properly,	La la la la la la la,
	La la la la la la la.
People make ath--umptionth.	La la la la la la la,
	La la la la la la la.
I want lessons	La la la la la la,
	La la la la la la,
To learn how to	La la la la la la.
Play the thaxaphone	
Like my brother.	
I have lessons	
To learn how to	
Thay "the thaxaphone"	
Like my brother.	

Ass   When you're in a donkey's head
They think that you are praying.
When I should've said "amen"
I was shouting *bum-flaps*.
People all should wear these heads,
'Cause in a donkey's head they would not
Give a monkey's what they ever
Said to one another.

Ass	**Wise Frankincense**
	If
BUM	
	I

POO

CRAP

BOOBS

FART

MY

DOG'S

GOT

A

RED (*Pause*)
WILLY.

Learn

To

Say

"Frankinthenth" I

Might

Learn

The

Thaxaphone.

Black-out

SCENE 5

The wings

Narrator races into the boys' wings

Narrator Adrian? *Adrian?*

Gabriel enters and emerges from behind Narrator

Gabriel Move.
Narrator (*turning*) Have you seen New Adrian? He's gone.
Gabriel Who?
Narrator New Adrian! Who has (*gesturing a "present"*) — y'know.
Gabriel Oh right. "Fankinthenth".

Narrator races off

Wise Gold races into the girls' wings

Wise Gold Adrian-n! *Adrian?*

Shepherd follows Wise Gold on

He's gone! New Adrian. With the frankincense an' it's your fault 'cause you laughed at him sayin' "prethenth".

Shepherd (*shrugging*) I didn't laugh at 'im. I just said that he said it.

Wise Gold (*copying a recent gesture*) She has HAD IT with this class, Mizz Horrocks. She has just HAD IT.

Wise Gold exits to look for New Adrian

Crossfade to Mrs Horrocks' special place during the following speech. Angel is in there, waiting in the dark

Shepherd (*matter of factly*) 'S the truth. You have to tell the truth. (*Calling*) It's what my mum says. (*Pausing to think a moment*) Then when I told Miss Horrocks it was Bradley who'd ate fifteen days chocolate out the advent calendar she said "No-one likes a tell-tale." An' that was the truth.

SCENE 6

Mrs Horrock's Special Place

Here, in the dark, is a huddled Angel

Wise Gold (*off*) Adriun-n. Adrian!

Wise Gold opens the door to the Special Place

Is Adrian in here?

Angel (*crying*) No.

Wise Gold closes the door

Wise Gold (*off*) Adrian-n.

Angel cries alone in the darkness a few moments

Wise Gold opens the door again

(*Tentatively*) Whas' the matter?

Angel (*gently crying*) I'm gonna get done.

Wise Gold Everyone is. She said if she has to put the overhead projector on we'd all get——

Angel By me mum.

Wise Gold (*frowning*) What, *she* thinks the singing's rubbish?

Angel (*snapping*) She gave it me, didn't she? (*Pause*) She gave it me. (*She sniffs*) 'S a present.

Wise Gold (*trying a smile; pointing*) "Lucky".

Angel looks round at her

If y' get things. If they give you things. Y'r mum. Y'r a "three ell". A "Lucky Little Lady". (*Holding up her "gift"*) I got "bath salts to combat stress". And there's a baby doll there with a little cot, which has got—

Angel (*with a "you don't understand" expression*) I didn't turn it on.

Wise Gold frowns. Apparently no, she doesn't understand

Just then was the bit when I should've turned it on. (*Anger rising again*) But if I turned it on it would've looked better 'n Ashley's and Ashley'll stop being friends because it'd be better 'n hers an' she's number one Angel and I don't *want it*. I don't *wannit*. It's only for my mum to stupid show-off back to Missis Vorbani.

Piano introduction to Music 8. starts

Wise Gold (*eyes wide*) Song! Wise men!

Wise Gold exits, leaving the door open

Angel remains, illuminated in the half-light, left with her thoughts

SCENE 7

The stage and Mrs Horrocks' Special Place

Narrator walks on

Narrator (*with great confidence*) At this time in the East there were Three Wise Men. One night a star appeared in the skies and they knew they must follow it.

Wise Gold enters, just making it on stage in time

Music 8. Lucky Lady

Everyone (*not Narrator, Wise Gold or Angel; off*)
                          We three kings of Orient are
                          Bearing gifts...
Wise Gold   Back home in the car
                          Did the king go to the bingo
                          Where Mum and me Grandma are?
                          Oh the baby doll that talks and sings
                          Golden hair in curly rings
                          I'm so lucky that my mummy
                          Tries so hard to win me things.

Everyone else   Larr larr larr larr larr la larr.

The Lights dim on Narrator

The Lights brighten on Angel in Mrs Horrocks' Special Place

Angel   Just for daddy's little princess
                       Here's a gift to go with your dress
                       Bring it on! Girl, there's no-one in the
                       World that we won't impress!

*She presses a button up her sleeve. A red chaser light comes on around the
rim of her wings, like the front of a cheap disco*

                       Oh-h... (*breaking her heart, singing*)
                       Other Angels' wings are white,
                       Yours do red from left to right'.
                       If I'm daddy's little princess
                       That makes dad a king tonight.

Everyone else   Larr larr larr larr larr la.

The Lights brighten on Narrator

Narrator   My dad picks me up from school
                       My dad picks me... (*petering out*)
                       My dad isn't there at breakfast,
                       But he's always there at school.
                       Oh-h...   **Wise Gold**   **Angel**

Narrator	**Wise Gold**	**Angel**
Every night	She comes with a cot	Down and Up
He comes and picks me Up from School	Cool little cot	Then winks on and off
	Lucky lady	Little princess
My dad picks me Up from school	Lucky lady..	Little princess........

My dad picks me up from...

Gabriel throws open the door like Cruella

A clap of thunder

Black-out on the stage

SCENE 8

The Lights up on Mrs Horrocks' Special Place

Gabriel Was she speaking to you?

Angel jumps and fumbles for her light switch so the chaser lights go off

Before? In here? Was she talking to you?
Angel (*swallowing*) Er ...
Gabriel Right. (*She points for Angel to leave*) We're not talking to her.
Angel Me?
Gabriel No, "her". I *am* talking to you.
Angel Oh right.
Gabriel Go on.

Angel bustles past with her awkward wings, knocking Mrs Horrocks' handbag off the door handle and exits

(*Giving a "come and pick it up" look*) Bag-g.

But Angel's gone. Aggrieved at having to do it, Gabriel picks it up. As she does, she has an idea. She looks at it. She puts it on her arm, like an adult

"I'm not havin' that." (*Pause. This makes her feel grown-up*) "I am *so* not having that." (*She looks in the bag, rummages, and pulls out a lipstick, which she applies, talking into a mirror as she does*) "If you want us we'll be in Brannigan's." (*Mm-mms the lipstick*) "Then off into town but look, I'll be on the moby." (*She peers into the bag again and deliciously pulls out a large tampon. She inspects it, unwraps it and puts it to her mouth like a cigarette; "smoking"*) Dave, if I want to stay overnight at Karen's I'll bloody well stay overnight at Karen's. I'm not having that stuck-up hag tell me what——

Angel enters

Angel Ashley. Have you got any juice? Jenny Bennet's had a bit of sick come up.

Music of "Joy to the World" and a golden light falls. Gabriel's world has been lit up

Gabriel Thank you, Jesus.

SCENE 9

Stage and wings

Shepherd is in the wings

Mary bustles on with Herod's crown

Mary It's not chickenpox.
Shepherd You 'ave to tell Mizz Horrocks.
Mary It was *coughing*.
Shepherd (*ever drawn to the visceral*) It was vomit.
Mary (*avoiding the issue with over-industriousness*) Now, where is he?
Shepherd I've seen vomit. One of the sheepdogs vomited once on the farm and it looked just like what you did only then the other sheepdogs ate it.
Star (*off*) Palace! Herod!

Star flies on stage to "erect" the "palace", clearly this is supposed to be done with Shepherd's help.

Shepherd (*following Star, casual as ever*) 'S the truth. Like me tellin' Bradley if he wants to marry you he'd have to make his hair nice and not go like John Burdgeon.
Mary Who?
Shepherd The fat man. Who was there with Mary and Joseph.

On the stage, Star and Shepherd are assembling the "palace", Narrator is in place

Narrator The palace of Herod was very big. It was full of gold and jewels.

Herod enters the wings

Mary Here he is! (*She puts on Herod's crown*)
Herod Where's me crown?
Mary What is he *like*?
Herod I was lookin' for that.

Mary (*mothering him to death*) You're not lookin' for anything! Y'r not doing anything properly!

Herod I'm doing it better n' you.

Mary Y'r not, 'cause my mum's done it with me and you're not doing anything of the looking up and makin' it look like proper acting like what y'see at The Empire or on television!

Herod (*frowning*) Y'do it like on the television?

Mary (*blurting*) *Yes*! Gerhumph!

Mary coughs up a bit of sick. They all look down at it on the floor

Wise Gold enters the stage from the Boys' wing

Wise Gold We are looking for a new baby king.

In the Girls' wings

Herod (*looking up at Mary*) That's puke.

On the stage

Narrator Herod came out of his palace.

Herod steps over the vomit and walks on to the stage

He didn't like it that there was a new king.

Herod does a "not like it" face, like a football manager on the touchline

He got very angry. He made——

Herod (*suddenly*; *very loudly*) Aaaargh. (*He decides to go for acting "like on the television". Which for him is largely football. He silently and slowly falls to the floor, as if fouled in an action replay*)

Narrator (*watching him in horror*) He made ...

Wise Gold and Narrator stand by powerless as Herod does a superb bit of the only "acting" he's ever witnessed — that of a stricken continental footballer. He rolls gently backwards, clutching his knee. He gestures for action from the ref's assistant, gesturing towards Wise Gold as the offender. Finally he starts mouthing the "F" word and sticking the "V"s up

(*Quickly*) He promised, (*looking at his crib cards quickly*) he made them — to promise — to find the new king and tell him. When they had. Then he sent them on their way.

Herod directs Wise Gold "off" by holding up a red card and pointing, like a football referee

Wise Gold exits to the wings, confused

Herod exits after her

But much later, long after the Wise Men had gone, Herod the king was still very worried.

In the girls' wings

Herod Oooof mmmm hmmmm (*He puts his hands behind his back and looks "worried"*)

On the stage

Narrator In the dead of night he came back and walked around the palace for many hours, thinking about what the Wise Men had said.

In the girls' wings

Herod climbs back towards the stage. Sadly, on the very first step he puts his foot inside his capacious gown. This means he actually steps inside his robe. The next step, he steps up further inside his robe. And the next. His body gets lower and lower, until by the top step, finally his chin is on his knees

Herod (*commentating*) Oh. He's in his cloak. He's in his cloak. (*Pauses slightly*) He's in trouble now, Gary. (*He rolls gently sideways off the back of the steps and disappears*)

Star whizzes in to the boys' wings

Star (*on high octane; to Narrator who is on stage*) I seen him! I seen him! Look at the back!
Narrator What?
Star Who's come!
Narrator I know! Me Mum an' Dad!
Star Me Uncle Ted! It was supposed to be tomorrow but he's come today! He works for NASA! (*Suddenly deadly serious*) He knows all about stars.

Star races off back into the toilets

Narrator The wise men went on for many days and nights. They followed the star until they reached the lowly stable. In here they knocked on the door. Inside they found Mary and Joseph with their new baby.

They reveal the stable containing Herod (now in his role as Joseph), a very bitter Mary, a beaming Gabriel, dressed as Mary, with copious make-up on, and two baby Jesus' in the crib

They were sitting peace... (*a beat, taking in the two-Mary situation*) ...peacefully round the manger.
Mary (*bitterly; across at Gabriel*) What y' doing?

Wise Gold enters

Wise Gold We are three kings.
Mary (*in a deathly whisper to Gabriel*) Get off.
Gabriel (*deathly whispering back*) No.
Wise Gold Have you just had a baby boy?
Herod (*looking at both babies*) Twins.
Wise Gold What is his name?
Herod (*suddenly realizing he's in a panel of three, and consequently in his element*) Can we confer?
Mary ⎫
Gabriel ⎭ (*together; "snap"*) *Jesus.*
Herod (*looking up*) Sue, we think his name's "Jesus".
Wise Gold We have brought gifts for him.
Mary ⎫
Gabriel ⎭ (*together; racing to say it first*) Thank you.
Wise Gold I bring him some gold. (*She walks forwards and puts it in front of the crib. Then goes back*)

There is of course no Wise Frankincense, which means there's an ugly pause

(*Walking forward again*) And I bring him some myrrh. (*She returns to her spot*)

An awkward pause. Then without warning

Wise Frankincense (*off*) And I bring him....

Wise Frankincense enters, stately as a galleon, as if he was Lazarus, raised from the dead. He has an air of coolness about him

He is accompanied by Ass, who waits in the boys' wings

And I bring him ...

There is a beat, in which resolve is summoned. Everyone's breath is held

(Sotto voce) ...Ssss–sss.... (*which finally produces*) More myrrh. (*He beams*) And I don't give a shit. (*He does a thumbs-up to Ass*)

Ass thumbs-up's him back

There is a flash of red teacher light

There is a crash from the piano to start Music 9

Angel enters the stage

Ass exits into the toilets

The final tableau is assembled — comprising: Gabriel, Herod, Mary, Shepherd, Wise Frankincense, Wise Gold, Angel, and Narrator, whose crowning moment this is for a supreme showing-off of of how well he's learned his lines

Music 9. Massive Newt

Everyone (*under*)
Silent night, holy night
Hum hum hum, hum hum hum,
Hum hum hum hum hum
Hum hum hum hum
Hum hum hum hum hum
Hum hum hum hum

Hum hum hum hum hum
Hum-hum

Hum hum hum
Hum hum hum hum.

Narrator (*speaking*)
The baby was a sign of happiness and peace.
Mary (*singing*) Round yon virgin Mother and child
Shepherd (*to Herod; speaking*) "Round John Burdgeon". Told you there was a fat bloke there an' all.
Narrator (*confidently; to his "Mum and Dad"*) A sign for children all over the world, that Jesus... (*peering out, he sees something and stops*)

Everyone looks at him

Various kids (*whispering urgently*) Timm-m!
Shepherd Tim, y' nugget-t! Stop lookin'.

From the wings on comes what looks like a walking bunch of flags. It is the Innkeeper. The "flags" are rigid, made of painted cardboard packaging sellotaped to bamboo canes. He hands them out

Everyone (*under*)
Hum hum hum hum,
Hum hum hum hum
Hum hum hum, hum hum hum,

Hum hum hum hum hum
Hum hum hum hum

Hum hum hum hum hum
Hum hum hum hum

Hum hum hum hum hum
Hum-hum

Hum hum hum
Hum hum hum hum.

Everyone
Silent night
Holy night
Hum hum hum
Hum hum hum

Shepherd
'S not allowed t' look at your mum an' dad.

Narrator (*gently*) I'm not. It's not me Dad she's come with.

We let this land, but his heartbreak is counterpointed by the final two flags being handed out and revealing:

Innkeeper   Right. Who gets France? (*He reveals his new hairdo. He has combed it flat with glue and consequently looks like something out of an eighties pop video. He smoothes it with Oliver Reed mischief, for Mary's benefit*)

Narrator   (*fighting back tears*) And finally... (*swallowing*) a sign appeared in the sky above them... (*breathing in for strength*) it was a sign of God's love for ever and ever. It was—the beautiful Star of Bethlehem.

Everyone turns to see the model star appear, but...

Up the steps from the wings, in gravity-free slow-motion rises Star dressed as an astronaut

Star (*making an intercom buzz noise*) Roger, Houston. Kk-kk. Over.

Houston calling Uncle Ted, over. (*Pointing from his vantage point at the back*) Overhead projector going on, over.

Everone on stage is suddenly smacked with white light, on which words have been scrawled. We see what they see, so it appears the children have indistinct writing all over their faces. It means suddenly everyone sings for the first time in unison, and as though suddenly the power's been turned on

Everyone (*singing*) Radiance beams from thy holy face

Suddenly, over the words, something moves with horror-movie litheness across all their faces

What's that climbing across the back wall?
Star (*pointing at the back wall; speaking*) Houston, we have Peter Crouch.

Everyone else points up.

Innkeeper ⎫
Mary ⎬ (*together; pointing; singing*) Great crested newt!
Gabriel (*as Mary*) Sleep in heavenly
               Sleep in heavenly

Everyone joins in , but at random times

Everyone (*randomly*) Sleep in heavenly
               Sleep in heavenly...

We go into slow-motion; everyone either rears up or scatters, or falls, or collides ... it's basically like watching the slow-motion of a bomb going off. As the carol echoes like a bad dream, Gabriel assumes the prominence she always wanted with Mary gone, only to be given a nose bleed by the turning wings of Angel. Wise Gold steps in to protect Angel from the retaliation of Gabriel

Gabriel tries to attack the unified Wise Gold and Angel (whose wings are now flashing a rather symbolic heart-outline) with the baby Jesus but is broadsided by other mayhem as the cast in slow motion fall, collapse and run for cover

Finally all we are left with on stage is the Star of Bethlehem, contemplating the spikey "star" headpiece

Star (*singing*)   Oh little town of Bethlehem
                         This ought to be over you

(*Beat. He turns the star*)
                        I should have stuck you up there on the rope
                        That's what I was told to do.
(*Beat. He holds the star up*)
                        But it's not a star,
                        Because a star is made of helium,
                        And hydrogen, magnesium
                        And sometimes iron too.
                        And this is just some stupid load of spikes
                        It looks like a baby drew.

                        But little kids draw stars with loads of spikes
                        'Cause that's how they look in books.
Everyone else (*off*) Silent night
Star   Like grown-ups don't want children growing up
                        To know how a real star looks.
Everyone else (*off*) Silent night
Star   Like my dad, he mustn't want me ever growin' up
                        Or else he'd let me visit NASA
                        And watch stars with Uncle Ted, (*pause*)
                        But I will grow, an' never make my son
                        Go camping in Wales
Everyone else (*off*) Silent
Star   To fish in a stream
Everyone else (*off*) Silent
Star   And watch rugby league instead.

*Star suddenly gets a message from the wings via the red teacher light. He
stands up, and puts the Bethlehem star on the rope hurriedly*

(*Speaking*) Mums and dads, Mizz Horrocks says no-one's hurt so can
everyone stay in the class an' sing the last verse.

*And with that: there is a key change in the music, and a moment of magic
as the adult voices start to be heard off, and as Star prepares to set the
spikey Bethlehem star swinging, we crossfade from the world of children*

SCENE 10

Mrs Horrocks' classroom — adult scale — the world of adults!

*From windows to wall paintings, everything is there in exactly the
place it was, but the size it would be in "normal, adult" life. The Star*

of Bethlehem which seemed so big a few seconds ago seems tiny now as it swings in the background. New additions on the walls we can see are some ground plans reading "Our New Hall"', and on the other side a large lizard photo headed "Rare Newts". Some cling-filmed jugs of post nativity hospitality are on a hotplate with mince pies

Singing from little photocopied sheets are the backs of the adults who we'll discover to be:
Mary's Mum, somewhere at the end of her thirties, dressed in M&S
Gabriel's Mum, twenties and dressed very young
Herod's Dad, forty, bluetooth earpiece, dressed for golf
Wise Frankinsence's Dad, forty, smart suit
Shepherd's Mum, later thirties, jumper and wellingtons
Innkeeper's Dad, early forties, grey suit and Lord Mayor's chain

Parents	Silent night, holy night
	Shepherds quake at the sight
	Glories stream from heaven afar
	Heavn'ly hosts sing "alleluia"
	Christ the Saviour is born
	Christ the Saviour is born.

As the song ends, there is a mêlée of adults

Mary's Mum is first to turn

Mary's Mum God Almighty. I'm glad OFSTED weren't in to see that.
Gabriel's Mum (*starting to sing*) "We wish you a merry"——
Mary's Mum Not yet! Not yet! Mulled wine first!
Herod's Dad So what d'you think of that then?
Wise Frankincense's Dad (*drily*) Well I'm sure the appearance of an astronaut will have pleased any Scientologists.
Mary's Mum Where's everyone gone?
Gabriel's Mum Which one was yours?
Innkeeper's Dad Shepherd and the Innkeeper.
Shepherd's Mum We had twins. Not identical. One of 'em's a little girl, the other one's a little sod.
Mary's Mum Yes. Look. (*Pointing to the programme; reading*) "Please remain in the classroom for hospitality". It's what the PTA decided. (*To herself*) All three of us.
Gabriel's Mum (*approaching Mary's mum*) That is lov-ely.
Mary's Mum (*nodding; politely*) Right. Thanks. M&S I'm afraid.
Gabriel's Mum (*helping; genuinely friendly*) No, I meant your top.

Mary's Mum (*beat*) I know.

Gabriel's Mum Oh right! Sorry! I thought you thought I meant the mulled wine! Sorry. I'm always doing that! Putting me foot in it. I didn't mean—I mean it's great. It's really snug. I've just bought one of them for me mum.

Mary's Mum takes a little hit, but it was totally innocent

Wise Frankincense's Dad (*sipping*) So what did you make of it?

Herod's Dad Crap. Absolute toss. Start to finish.

Wise Frankincense's Dad Sorry?

Herod's Dad I told Phil afterwards, it was the worst seminar I've ever been to. (*He moves past, holding his cellphone earpiece, smiling '"one minute" to Wise Frankincense's dad*)

Gabriel's Mum Please God I hope you weren't looking what the Angel Gabriel had on! I made it for this toga party last week. God, yours is *so* lucky having a mum who can sew.

Mary's Mum Well yours is lucky having an older sister who goes to toga parties

Gabriel's Mum No, no. I'm her mum. (*She moves away*)

For some reason this seems to hit Mary's Mum like a clawhammer

Angel's Mum enters: striking, svelte, glamorously-dressed, looking like some Bollywood star. She is carrying a tray of mince pies

Angel's Mum (*cooly*) And here she comes. From the east. Bearing mince pies. (*Pointing at the mince pies*) Dove. On the top. Sign of peace.

Herod's Dad (*returning to Wise Frankincense's Dad*) Sorry about that. These guys cannot get their heads round me having opted out.

Wise Frankincense's Dad Of what?

Herod's Dad My wife and I, we alternate. She has two years to pursue her career, I spend two caring for our son. Then we... (*gesturing "flip"*) ...

Angel's Mum (*meaning Mary's Mum*) Staying at home's a full time job. Ask superwoman.

Herod's Dad (*to Mary's Mum*) It's gold, isn't it? My wife's never back before eight and she misses it. All that quality time, early evening, just me and our Ryan. Way I see it, that is time you will never get ag... (*Loudly*) Andy-y!

Herod's Dad holds his ear and goes out for a better signal

Gabriel's Mum (*returning*) See, the *nice* dress she sneaked in with is *bought*, y'see. My husband — first wife, their daughter was in this class last year and 'course Mother now insists on all the whistles and bells.

Mary's Mum (*pointing*) Drink for Missis Horrocks.

Gabriel's Mum But *ta-da-a!* Guilt opens wallets. Daughter one gets Versace. Daughter two gets a bedsheet.

Mary's Mum (*lurching*) Not that one! Mrs Horrocks doesn't drink alcohol.

Gabriel's Mum (*frowning*) She just downed two of these in one!

Shepherd's Mum (*loudly*) Will you stop calling them "my people". They made you mayor, love, not emperor.

Angel's Mum (*passing Mary's Mum*) Sarah. Just took a call from your husband in the office.

Mary's Mum Really?

Angel's Mum He's having to work late.

Wise Frankincense's Dad (*reading the little flag in his mince pie*) More mince pies. "marinaded in sherry with a cinnamon crust". Courtesy of a Mrs "Vorbani".

Angel's Mum (*coolly; on it like a hawk*) Sorry?

Wise Frankincense's Dad Rather striking indian lady.

Angel's Mum Mrs Vorbani?

Wise Gold's Mum enters carrying a wildly crying baby doll in swaddling clothes

Mary's Mum (*thinking the doll is a real baby*) Oh good Lord!

Mary's Mum } (*together*) { What can I get? Do you need...?
Wise Gold's Mum } { No, it's OK. It's OK. It's OK...

Mary's Mum (*flapping*) D'you need something warming? Will she have some milk?

Wise Gold's Mum No, no it's all right. I'll be able to shut her up with a screwdriver.

Mary's Mum Sorry?

Wise Gold's Mum Or a knife? (*Giving a "have you got a" look*) Long sharp knife? (*She turns the doll upside down by one leg and peers at the back*) Just get the bloody batteries out.

Wise Frankincense's Dad (*taking the doll*) I've something on my keys.

Wise Frankincense's Dad moves away

Wise Gold's Mum Oh you angel. (*To Mary's Mum*) What is she like? Straight out of the packet, presses the bloody — thanks (*she takes a mulled wine*) — bloody prods it, little 'mare. She's hamfisted, see. She's like her dad. Hands like a bloody gibbon. Mind you, she's excited.

Shepherd's Mum Was that for tonight?

Wise Gold's Mum (*swallowing wine; nodding*) Mg. Fantastic. Best ever!

Mary's Mum Wasn't it! There's something about a nativity that——

Wise Gold's Mum (*listing her winnings*) That doll, a set of power tools and then, only got a "Fastest to Four Corners" bonus, won a bloody wicker basket of body oils! I mean "Christmas"? I'm half-done now, for the rellys! (*Beat*) How *was* the nativity?

Wise Frankincense's Dad returns with a quietened doll

Shepherd's Mum A cracker. Someone's stick insect got on the overhead projector and came up the size of Godzilla.
Wise Frankincense's Dad Don't forget the astronaut.

Star's "Dad" enters

Star's "Dad" Wasn't that brilliant?

Everyone turns to look at Star's "Dad" who is suddenly there!

Wasn't that just *completely* amazing? To link "star" with the concept of "astronaut"? That is down-the-line quantum association.
Mary's Mum (*politely, as ever*) I hadn't thought, but when you look at it... (*She offers a drink to Star's "Dad"*) I can see why he's got a proud dad! Do you——?
Star's "Dad" (*freezing*) Is he here? (*Pause*) The astronaut's dad?

They all look at him. There's a pause

Mary's Mum Sorry, you are ...?
Star's "Dad" Ted. "Uncle". Well, he calls me "Uncle". I'm just a friend, really. His (*nodding*) mother and I were at Hope University together.
Mary's Mum R-right. Before she got m——
Star's "Dad" —pregnant.
Mary's Mum Married.
Star's "Dad" Anyway.
Wise Gold's Mum (*a bit drunk; pointing at a painting*) Have you seen these nativities? (*Pointing at another painting*) They are crap some of these, bless 'em.
Star's "Dad" (*in a parting shot, as though she needs to know*) He's very bright.
Wise Gold's Mum This kid's done Mary, Joseph then a right fat bloke who looks like John Prescott.
Mary's Mum (*trying to stop Wise Gold's Mum messing with the paintings*) Excuse me ...

Herod's Dad returns from his phone call

Herod's Dad (*rubbing his hands*) So anyway! How's this mulled wine...? (*Putting his hand to his ear*) Phil-l!

Herod's Dad walks straight back out again

Wise Gold's Mum (*taking a picture off the wall*) Duck With An Ice Cream! Bloody hell, they have their work cut out with some of these kids, the teachers.

Mary's Mum tries to return the painting to its wall. Angel's Mum, super sleek, coolly and methodically bins Mrs Vorbani's mince pies

Angel's Mum That is such a coincidence. (*Calling to Mary's Mum*) Sarah! Until recently the new boy's dad has been working in the Far East!

Wise Frankincense's Dad (*quickly covering*) And as I was saying it's one of your problems in a state school, being tied to council contractors. Private sector, there's no way that hall wouldn't be up now.

Wise Gold's Mum Fantastic mince pies.

Angel's Mum (*to Wise Frankincense's Dad*) Problem was she saw Joseph's Dreamcoat, you see. With all the colours. And of course she wanted her wings like THAT. And she *pestered* and *pestered* ...

Mary's Mum Yours was the child with the ...?

Wise Frankincense's Dad (*brutally*) With the lisp.

Mary's Mum (*quietly*) Frankincense.

Ass' Dad enters dressed as Santa Claus in a shabby red fat-suit and beard and hat

Ass' Dad Ho ho ho! Merry Christmas, everybody!

Mary's Mum Hold on, hold on. I don't think we booked this.

Ass' Dad (*stopping dead*) It's all right, in't it? This? I know it's not like "religious" but it's just—last Friday before Christmas I always borrow the delivery truck for handing out presents for the kiddies. Y'know? Round us?

Mary's Mum You've watched the whole nativity like that?

Ass' Dad (*proudly*) He was the donkey.

Innkeeper's Dad (*pointing*) Delivery truck from work? Oh right, are these Rotary Club presents?

Ass' Dad No no. Just me. I buy 'em meself, off the market.

Innkeeper's Dad (*pointing dramatically at Ass' Dad*) That is what this town is missing. This is what I want to bring back to this town.

Shepherd's Mum Love, you're the mayor. Y've only got jurisdiction over the siting of bus stops.

Innkeeper's Dad (*shaking Ass' Dad's hand; in a posh voice*) I'm in the food and wine business.

Shepherd's Mum We run a pub.

Innkeeper's Dad That does paninis.

Shepherd's Mum (*with a very posh voice*) Thanks to my father dying I've suddenly inherited the family farm so I'm now in the "left arm up a sheep's arse" business.

Innkeeper's Dad (*sweeping her away*) Can I have a word?

Gabriel's Mum enters with glasses. During the following, Herod's Dad returns

Gabriel's Mum Refills for Miss Horrocks!

Mary's Mum Look we really need to get people back...

Wise Frankincense's Dad (*to Angel's Mum*) ...My son recently developed a speech-anomaly and *immediately* this school is all "oh we'll bolster his confidence by putting him in the learning support unit". (*Including Ass' Dad too*) Don't put him in some bloody unit with a load of drongos who are just going to make him feel better about being abnormal. Am I right?

Ass' Dad (*pausing; staring at him*) God, your poor son.

Innkeeper's Dad (*whispering to his wife*) I'm sorry, but having Travellers on that field breaks up a town's sense of community.

Mary's Mum (*passing, gives Ass' Dad a drinking straw*) Straw. So it doesn't stain your beard.

Innkeeper's Dad (*grabbing Ass' Dad and putting an arm round him*) What you need is more people who are willing to go out and bond, like him.

Ass' Dad Oh aye. Bonding's a big thing for us. But then I s'pose it would be, wouldn't it? A lot of communities haven't got much time for us Travellers.

Shepherd's Mum (*patting Innkeeper's Dad on the back; making a pratfall-noise*) Wac— wa–ack.

Gabriel's Mum Look at her!

Mary's Mum turns

Y'r just a natural mother, aren't you? Y' cope with anything. I still feel — honest to God — I come in that lounge some days and Ashley's sitting there an' I think: "Oh God I had a kid, didn't I?!"

Shepherd's Mum (*addressing the hymn sheets*) Right, are we doing this or what?

Gabriel's Mum Sometimes I don't know why he married me.

Mary's Mum In my experience, probably because his first wife turned into a "natural mother".

Shepherd's Mum (*trying to jump start the singing*) We wish ...

Mary's Mum Not yet. Can you tell people ...

Angel's Mum (*collecting people's mince pies*) Can you tell people?
Mary's Mum What?
Wise Gold's Mum (*pointing next door*) In there?
Mary's Mum Yes. *No.*
Angel's Mum Some of these are sub-standard.
Mary's Mum In HERE. (*To Angel's Mum*) What?
Herod's Dad (*heading out*) We going in there?
Innkeeper's Dad (*meaning the wine jugs*) Can we have another spice bag?
Mary's Mum (*to both questions*) No. No.
Angel's Mum (*showing her some mince pies*) Ones with the dove of peace.
Innkeeper's Dad (*fishing a mulled wine sachet out of a jug*) Give it here.
Mary's Mum (*politely trying to stop him*) It's one per jug!
Innkeeper's Dad Like chucking a teabag in Lake Windermere.
Wise Frankincense's Dad So what's the plan then?
Wise Gold's Mum We're not singing.
Mary's Mum No, we ARE ...
Herod's Dad Now?
Mary's Mum No ...
Wise Frankincense's Dad Which verses?
Herod's Dad (*singing*) We wish ...
Mary's Mum Not yet.
Shepherd's Mum (*fighting with Innkeeper's Dad over the wine jugs*) That's too strong!
Innkeeper's Dad That's too weak.
Ass' Dad Yo ho ho!
Herod's Dad (*singing*) We wish...
Gabriel's Mum Not yet.
Herod's Dad (*looking at his watch*) It's gonna be Easter.
Wise Frankincense's Dad Who starts?
Herod's Dad Ask superwoman.
Angel's Mum (*pointing*) Wrong pie!
Wise Gold's Mum In here?
Shepherd's Mum Put that back!
Innkeeper's Dad No!
Wise Frankincense's Dad Who starts?
Mary's Mum (*too loud*) *I don't know!*

Silence. That WAS loud

I'm not in charge, all right? I'm pouring wine, I'm holding trays but I'm not—can I just say—I absolutely—I wish I was. I wish—I really—(*starting to cry*) I wish I was.

Mary's Mum exits

Music 10. starts

Everyone else in the classroom is left slightly stunned

Gabriel's Mum (*stepping into the breach*) Come on, everyone, there
we go.

Music 10. I Wish

Everyone (*joining in the music in dribs and drabs*)
        We wish you a merry Christmas
        We wish you a merry Christmas
        We wish you a merry Christmas
        And a happy New Year.

Gabriel's Mum manages to gets everyone singing

        Good tidings we bring
        To you and your kin
        Or king
        Or something.
        And a happy New Year.

*Exactly as happened with the children, the parents are isolated with their
thoughts*

Innkeeper's Dad (*to the tune "Hark the Herald"*)
        I wish that I ran a rest'raunt
        Egon Ronay, Michelin-starred
        Currently I just knee people
        In the balls and say "You're barred".

Everyone We wish you a merry Christmas
        We wish you a merry Christmas
        We wish you a merry Christmas
        And a happy New Year.

Herod's Dad (*to the tune "Once in Royal"*)
        I hope that my wife will honour
        The career deal that we made.
        All the hours of boring board games
        All the damn Kerplunk that I have played.
        This year I spent with our son
        Next year she gets all this bloody fun.

Shepherd's Mum (*to the tune "While Sheperd's Watched"*)

I hope she runs for parliament
I hope he runs a car
Mechanics. Gym. Or anythin'
Except our sodding farm

Everyone We wish you a merry Christmas
We wish you a merry Christmas
We wish you a merry Christmas
And a happy new...
Wise Gold's Mum (*to the tune "We Three Kings"*)
Christmas time — I hope that she sees
Time's the gift that won't grow on trees.
Not all mums give up their Thursdays
To win her a doll that pees.

Angel's Mum (*shaking her head as if in woe*)
Ohh what a careless, CARELESS sin
Thirty mince pies in the bin
If I'd just taken one bite, it would look as if
People had tried them and then SPAT them in.

Wise Frankincense's Dad	**Ass' Dad**
(*to the tune "Ding Dong Merrily"*)	
I	Can only live in
Hope	That no-one rings
My	Delivery
Son	Day night, so I
Won't	Miss out on him
Think	...ing I'm Santa Claus.
Daddy is a failure.	

Gabriel's Mum (*descant to the tune "Away in a Manger"*)
I just hope, 'cause of how it goes
With a husband's first wife
That the daughter with no guilt clause
Doesn't spend her whole life (*slowing,* colla voce)
Trying to be Mary when she should realize
That in fact she is an angel...

The last line she can't quite get out, and is filled in by humming from the others

Everyone else *Hmm...*

Crossfade to the playground

SCENE 11

The playground

The Lights come up on Mary's Mum. She is sitting on the climbing frame, lost in the night

Mary's Mum (*to the tune "Away in a Manger"*)
>I wish he was dead
>I wish he was here
>I wish I hadn't redialled
>Heard her voice in my ear
>If I'd spent less time on children
>I wish that I knew
>But I wish most of all I remembered being twenty-two.

Music continues underscore

Narrator's Dad enters

Narrator's Dad Hallo?

Mary's Mum starts; turns

Are you with the nativity?
Mary's Mum (*wiping her eyes*) Sorry.
Narrator's Dad Just—y'know Tim? Lad who was the Narrator? Could you just, (*swallowing*) just tell him he was great, yeah? That he looked great. I was at the window. His dad. That I was really proud of him.

There's a moment

Mary's Mum You should tell him yourself.
Narrator's Dad Yeah it's—awkward. His mum and me are splitting up and we haven't told him yet. He doesn't know anything's wrong.
Mary's Mum (*squaring with him*) He's a seven-year-old child. He will have known before you did.

Everyone else (*off*) We wish you a merry Christmas
>We wish you a merry Christmas

> We wish you a merry Christmas
> And a happy New Year.

Mary's Mum looks at Narrator's Dad, to one in a war, from one about to fight it

Mary's Mum Come on. I'll take you in.

She stands and leads him inside

Crossfade to the classroom

SCENE 12

Mrs Horrocks' Classroom

The classroom singing grows in volume, picking up the pace again

Everyone (*growing in volume*) We wish you a merry Christmas
> We wish you a merry Christmas
> We wish you a merry Christmas
> And a happy New Year.
>
> We wish you a merry Christmas
> We wish you a merry Christmas
> We wish you a merry Christmas
> And a happy New Year.
>
> Glad tidings we bring
> To you and your kin
> We wish you a merry Christmas
> And a happy New Year!
>
> Glad tidings we bring
> To you and your kin
> We wish you a merry Christmas

Mary's Mum and Narrator's Dad enter at the back

And a hap...	**Mary's Mum** (*calling over the music*)
	Could we just have a bit of help in
...py....	the car park? Miss Horrocks has
	collapsed in the sand pit

Group 1 New Year........   **Group 2** We wish you a merry Christmas
                                                We wish you a merry Christmas
                                                We wish you a merry Christmas

Herod's Dad (*under the singing; taking a call; holding his Bluetooth ear*)
    I'm in a nativity. (*Nodding*) Yeah, 's great. (*Nodding*) Really brings it
    home.
Everyone (*singing; 5 part harmony*)
    And a happy new year.

BLACK-OUT

FURNITURE AND PROPERTY LIST

ACT I
SCENE 1

On stage: Giant teacher's chair
Giant swing bin
Stage upstage. *On it*: Home Corner with practical door and curtains at window
Classroom tables and chairs
Nature table with wheels. *On it*: plastic tank for stick insects
Astronaut suit with sign "Marcus's uncle works for NASA" and photos illustrating this
Model space shuttle
Large children's paintings of the nativity on one wall with writing as script
Cornflake box
Roll of silver foil
Egg carton
Large silver sprayed cardboard star on a hook (for **Star**)
Plastic bottle wrapped in crepe paper
Baby Jesus doll (oversized head and goony-faced), brush, comb (for **Mary**)

Off stage: Baby Jesus doll wrapped in a shawl and comb (**Angel** and **Wise Gold**)
Spanish straw donkey on wheels with lascivious wink and sombrero (**Shepherd**)
Box of All Gold chocolates, ornate plastic container of bath salts in bag (**Wise Gold**)

Personal: **Narrator**: large cardboard pieces with words (used throughout)
Mary: comb
Shepherd: comb
Gabriel: ripped-out piece from an illustrated bible

SCENE 2

No props required

SCENE 3

On stage: As SCENE 1

Set: Curtains across stage area to exits L and R
                Rope elevated across stage

SCENE 4

On stage: As previous scene

Off stage: Spanish straw donkey on wheels with lascivious wink and som-
                brero (**Mary** and **Herod**)

Personal: **Mary**: recorder
                Innkeeper: tooth

SCENE 5

On stage: Sections of brightly painted playground apparatus in playground
                area

SCENE 6

On stage: As SCENE 4

SCENE 7

On stage: As previous scene

Off stage: Spanish straw donkey on wheels with lascivious wink and som-
                brero (**Herod**)

Personal: **Star**: star on his head

ACT II
SCENE 1

On stage: As previous scene

Off stage: Haybale and goony-faced baby Jesus doll (**Ass**)
                Sheep (**Shepherd**)

SCENE 2

Off stage: Glue (**Star**)

SCENE 3

On stage: As ACT II, SCENE 1

Off stage: Spanish straw donkey on wheels with lascivious wink and sombrero (**Herod**)
Goony-faced baby Jesus doll with detachable head (**Mary**)

SCENE 4

On stage: Sections of brightly painted playground apparatus in playground area

Personal: **Ass**: Co-op bag on foot

SCENE 5

No props required

SCENE 6

On stage: Mrs Horrocks' handbag on door handle containing lipstick, tampon

Off stage: Ornate plastic container of bath salts (**Wise Gold**)

SCENE 7

On stage: Mrs Horrocks' handbag on door handle containing lipstick, tampon

SCENE 8

On stage: As previous scene

SCENE 9

On stage: Items for Herod's palace
                2 baby Jesus' in crib

Off stage: **Herod**'s crown (**Mary**)
                Box of All Gold chocolates, ornate plastic container of bath salts
                    (**Wise Gold**)
                Plastic bottle wrapped in crepe paper (**Wise Frankincense**)
                Cardboard flags sellotaped to garden canes (**Innkeeper**)
                Large silver sprayed cardboard star on a hook (**Star**)

Personal: **Narrator**: cards

SCENE 10

Strike: All items

Set: Normal size tables. *On one*: cling-filmed jugs of mulled wine,
                    mulled wine sachets, glasses, hotplate with mince pies, drinking
                    straws
                Normal size chairs
                Normal size children's paintings of nativity, large size ground
                    plans reading "Our New Hall", large lizard photo headed "Rare
                    Newts" on walls
                Small size star hanging from rope across the daïs

Off stage: Small photocopied programmes (**Parents**)
                Tray of mince pies with little flags in them (**Angel's Mum**)
                Battery operated crying doll in swaddling clothes (**Wise Gold's
                    Mum**)
                Glasses (**Gabriel's Mum**)

Personal: **Herod's Dad**: mobile phone earpiece

SCENE 11

On stage: Sections of brightly painted playground apparatus in playground
                area

SCENE 12

On stage: As ACT II, SCENE 10

Personal: **Herod's Dad**: mobile phone earpiece

LIGHTING PLOT

Property fittings required: nil
Various interior and exterior settings

ACT I, Scene 1

To open: lighting on front cloth

Cue 1	As the front cloth rises *Sharp focus white spot on group*	(Page 1)
Cue 2	**Innkeeper**: "I didn't. I never ——" *Snap white spot to red*	(Page 2)
Cue 3	**Innkeeper**: "Sorry, Missis Horrocks." *Snap red spot to white*	(Page 2)
Cue 4	**Innkeeper**: "Never." *Momentary white spot to red then back to white*	(Page 2)
Cue 5	**Shepherd**: "… load of — shttp." *Snap white spot to red then back to white*	(Page 2)
Cue 6	**Innkeeper** (singing): "… let us shout." *Snap white spot to red on* **Innkeeper**; *revert to white* *spot as he exits*	(Page 4)
Cue 7	**Everyone**: "Mrs Horrocks! Mrs Horrocks ..." *Crossfade to full, general interior lighting*	(Page 4)
Cue 8	**Everyone** stands for a moment to ruminate *Snap to white spot*	(Page 17)
Cue 9	**Everyone**: "Mizziz Horrocks! *White spot to red spot*	(Page 17)
*Cue*10	Silence *Red spot to white spot*	(Page 17)
Cue 11	**Gabriel**: "Yes, Missis Horrocks." *Crossfade to full, general interior lighting*	(Page 17)

Cue 12	**Angel** is horror-stricken *Snap to white spot*	(Page 22)

Cue 13	Dark music of evil a-doing *Black-out*	(Page 22)

ACT I, Scene 2

To open: Dim light on Mrs Horrocks' special place

Cue 14	**Star**: Now I am a man as well." *Black-out*	(Page 25)

ACT I, Scene 3

To open: Full, general interior lighting

No cues

ACT I, Scene 4

To open: Lighting on stage area and girls' and boys' wings

ACT I, Scene 5

To open: General daylight on playground area

No cues

ACT I, Scene 6

To open: When ready, bring up lighting in girls' wings

Cue 15	**Angel**: " … really Santa Claus?" *Bring up lighting on boys' wings*	(Page 34)

ACT I, Scene 7

To open: Lighting on stage area and girls' and boys' wings

Cue 16	**Star**: "Nope, Buzz Aldrin's in that ——" *Snap on red spot momentarily*	(Page 36)

Cue 17   **Innkeeper**: "You …" Horror-movie sting   (Page 37)
               Black-out

ACT II, SCENE 1

To open: Lighting on stage area and girls' and boys' wings

Cue 18   **Innkeeper**: "But he can bugger off."   (Page 38)
               Snap on red spot

Cue 19   **Innkeeper** disappears through the door backwards   (Page 38)
               Snap off red spot

Cue 20   **Shepherd** (speaking) "Thank you."   (Page 41)
               Black-out

ACT II, SCENE 2

To open: Dim lighting on Mrs Horrocks' special place

Cue 21   Door opens   (Page 42)
               Bring up lighting on **Innkeeper**

ACT II, SCENE 3

To open: Lighting on stage area

Cue 22   **Shepherd**: "Too late."   (Page 44)
               Black-out

ACT II, SCENE 4

To open: General evening light on playground area

Cue 23   **Ass**: "WILLY."   (Page 48)
               Black-out

ACT II, SCENE 5

To open: Lighting on girls' and boys' wings

Cue 24   **Shepherd**: "Then when I told Miss Horrocks …"   (Page 49)
               *Start crossfade to Mrs Horrocks' special place for
                   next scene*

ACT II, Scene 6

To open: Very dim lighting on Mrs Horrocks' special place

No cues

ACT II, Scene 7

To open: Lighting on stage area

| Cue 25 | **Everyone else**: "… larr larr la larr." | (Page 51) |
| | *Dim lighting on stage area and bring up subdued lighting on* **Angel** *in Mrs Horrocks' special place* | |

| Cue 26 | **Everyone else**: "…larr larr larr la." | (Page 51) |
| | *Bring up lighting on* **Narrator** | |

| Cue 27 | **Gabriel** throws open the door like Cruella | (Page 51) |
| | *Black-out* | |

ACT II, Scene 8

To open: Subdued lighting on **Angel** in Mrs Horrocks' special place

| Cue 28 | **Angel**: " … bit of sick come up." | (Page 52) |
| | *Golden light on* **Gabriel** | |

ACT II, Scene 9

To open: General lighting on stage area and boys' and girls' wings

| Cue 29 | **Ass** gives **Wise Frankincense** a thumbs-up sign | (Page 57) |
| | *Flash of red spot* | |

| Cue 30 | **Star**: "Overhead projector going on. Over." | (Page 58) |
| | *Bright white light with indistinct writing and moving dark stick-like object on children; fade when ready* | |

| Cue 31 | **Star**: "And watch rugby league instead." | (Page 60) |
| | *Flash of red spot* | |

ACT II, SCENE 10

To open: General interior lighting

No cues

ACT II, SCENE 11

To open: Night exterior lighting

No cues

ACT II, SCENE 12

To open: General interior lighting

No cues

EFFECTS PLOT

ACT I

Cue 1   When ready   (Page 1)
Tambourine shake and slap

Cue 2   **Innkeeper**: "I didn't. I never ——"   (Page 2)
Tambourine shake and slap

Cue 3   **Innkeeper**: "Never."   (Page 2)
Tambourine shake and slap

Cue 4   **Shepherd**: "… load of — shttp."   (Page 2)
Tambourine shake and slap

Cue 5   **Innkeeper** (singing): "… let us shout."   (Page 4)
Tambourine shake and slap

Cue 6   The Home Corner door opens   (Page 8)
Door creaks

Cue 7   They all turn. The door opens   (Page 16)
Door creaks

Cue 8   **Innkeeper**: "And the sherry." The door closes   (Page 16)
Door creaks

Cue 9   **Everyone**: "Mizziz Horrocks …"   (Page 17)
Tambourine shake and slap

Cue 10   **Mary** carries on tidying. The door opens   (Page 18)
Door creaks

Cue 11   The music stops   (Page 24)
Door creaks

Cue 12   **Star**: "Nope, Buzz Aldrin's in that ——"   (Page 36)
Tambourine shake and slap

ACT II

Cue 13   **Innkeeper**: "But he can bugger off."   (Page 38)
           Tambourine shake and slap

Cue 14   **Gabriel** throws open the door like Cruella   (Page 51)
           Clap of thunder

Cue 15   **Angel**: " … bit of sick come up."   (Page 52)
           Music: "Joy to the World"

Cue 16   **Ass** gives **Wise Frankincense** a thumbs-up sign   (Page 57)
           Tambourine shake and slap

Cue 17   **Star**: "And watch rugby league instead."   (Page 60)
           Tambourine shake and slap